MW00423652

SPIRIT *within*

&

THE
SPIRIT

upon

THE JOSEPH FAMILY

THE
SPIRIT *within*
&

THE
SPIRIT *upon*

The Holy Spirit's Twofold Work for the Believer

BY KENNETH E. HAGIN

15 14 13 12 11 10 09   11 10 09 08 07 06 05

The Spirit Within and the Spirit Upon
ISBN-13: 978-0-89276-533-1
ISBN-10: 0-89276-533-X

In the U.S. write:
Kenneth Hagin Ministries
P.O. Box 50126
Tulsa, OK 74150-0126
1-888-28-FAITH
www.rhema.org

In Canada write:
Kenneth Hagin Ministries
P.O. Box 335, Station D
Etobicoke (Toronto), Ontario
Canada, M9A 4X3
1-866-70-RHEMA
www.rhemacanada.org

CONTENTS

Chapter One

The Dual Working of the Holy Spirit |

There is an experience for the Christian subsequent to his New Birth experience. After a person has accepted Jesus Christ as Savior and is baptized into the Body of Christ as a member of God's family, another experience awaits him that will bring him deeper into the things of God, into a deeper dimension spiritually. That experience is the baptism in the Holy Spirit.

Believers have been confused about this subsequent experience, and theologians and church leaders have debated the subject throughout the centuries. I myself once believed that the work of the Spirit ended with one's being baptized into Christ—with being born again. Yet from the Bible, we can clearly see two separate and distinct workings, which I will endeavor to show in the pages of this book. I will also show the purpose for this dual-working of the Spirit of God: the Spirit *within* us in the New Birth for *character*, and the Spirit *upon* us in the baptism of the Holy Spirit for *service*.

My Own Experience

I received the Holy Spirit in the New Birth, just as you did if you are born again. With my Baptist background (I started out as a Baptist boy preacher pastoring a country church), I wasn't around Pentecostal people. There was no Pentecostal church in our town. There might have been some Pentecostal folks there, but I didn't know about them.

I was healed in 1934 of an incurable blood disease and a deformed heart. In 1935, someone came to our town, put up a tent, and began holding what he called a "Full Gospel revival." "Full Gospel" didn't mean anything to me. I was very busy and didn't go at first. But when I found out that they taught divine healing, I went! They got 465 people saved, and some of those people put up a building and called it the Full Gospel Tabernacle.

Regarding divine healing, I'd been standing alone as just a teenager. And it strengthened me to be around people who believed in the power of God in the areas of healing and faith. That's the reason I went to their meetings. They added to me; they helped me. But these people also taught this experience of being baptized in the Holy Spirit.

Now these Pentecostal folks didn't get anyone baptized in the Holy Ghost during this series of services. Their purpose was evangelistic, and the speakers preached evangelistic messages. The meeting ran eight weeks, and after about four weeks, they started having healing services a couple of nights each week.

Then during the last week, they started preaching a little about the baptism in the Holy Spirit, but no one received it. There weren't any workers present to help. After the group began meeting in the tabernacle, people started receiving that experience. I closed my ears to it, though. I thought, *I believe in the Holy Ghost, but I don't know about that "tongues" business. But I'll put up with a little fanaticism to have fellowship around faith and healing.* That's as far as I went at first.

But like a fellow down in east Texas said, "It's sort of like standing on a slippery creek bank. If you keep hanging around, you'll slip in." And I did. On April 8, 1937, at eight minutes past six p.m., in the living room of the Full Gospel Tabernacle pastor's house, I was baptized in the Holy Ghost and spoke with other tongues as the Spirit of God gave utterance!

My Baptist colleagues had warned me against this when they saw me hanging around those Pentecostal people. One fellow in particular in our church warned me. He was not an ordained minister of the Gospel, but he was a Bible teacher and taught the main Bible class in our church.

This man was a graduate of a major Bible seminary and had the same training as all the ministers who graduated from that school. We had quite a bit of fellowship together, and I remember him saying to me more than once, "I'll admit that those Pentecostal people in some ways are thoroughly orthodox in their beliefs. And I'll admit that those people down at the Full Gospel Tabernacle live better lives—cleaner and purer—than our people at the Baptist church do. But that speaking with tongues is of the devil!"

I thought, *How did those people get something from the devil that helps them to live better lives than the average*

*Christian? I never knew of the devil helping anyone to
live better. He usually helps them to be meaner.*

Well, this man was a seminary graduate, and I was
just a teenager, so I listened to him. But after I received
this Pentecostal experience, I remembered he said,
"That's not the Holy Spirit. It's some other kind of
spirit." (And the way the Pentecostals taught, they left
the impression that you didn't even *have* the Holy
Spirit in your life until you were baptized in the Holy
Ghost and spoke with tongues.)

But when I was baptized in the Holy Spirit and
spoke with tongues for an hour and a half, one of the
first things I realized was this: the Spirit giving me
utterance to speak in other tongues was the same Spirit
I got acquainted with three years earlier in the New
Birth. I didn't get a new or different spirit. The Holy
Ghost is not twins. He's just one Spirit. There are
different works of the Spirit, but just one Spirit.

So I kept on the lookout for that Baptist Sunday
school teacher. I knew he'd engage me in conversation
and warn me again about tongues being of the devil,
because he did that every time. I crossed his path again
purposely, and we started a conversation. I wanted him
to hurry up, so I brought the subject up myself. I said,
"You know that Pentecostal experience—that speaking
in tongues—these Full Gospel people talk about?"

"Yes," he said.

"You've been telling me that it's of the devil," I said.

"Oh, yes, it sure is!"

"Well, how do you know?"

"It's just not the same Spirit," he said. "It's not the Holy Ghost. We have the Holy Ghost come to us in the New Birth. That's a different spirit."

"It is?" I asked.

"Yes."

"Well," I continued, "if that Pentecostal experience of speaking with tongues that they have down there at the Full Gospel Tabernacle is of the devil, then the whole Southern Baptist movement is of the devil."

"What are you talking about?" he asked.

I said, "I've been baptized in the Holy Ghost and have spoken in other tongues! Oh, but don't be afraid. Nothing is going to get on you. The Holy Ghost is a gentleman. The same Spirit that I got acquainted with in the Southern Baptist church when I was born again is the One Who gave me utterance in tongues."

"Aw, no. That can't be so!" he said.

"Have you ever spoken with tongues?" I asked.

"No."

"How do you know, then?"

"Well, I just know it couldn't be so!" he replied.

"You're a seminary graduate, aren't you?" I asked.

"Oh, yes!"

"Then you know the Bible says that a man who answers before he hears a matter is a fool [Prov. 18:13]. Don't be a fool. If you've never spoken with tongues, how do you know what Spirit it is?"

I continued, "You see, I have the New Birth, the born-again experience, and I have this experience too. I ought to know."

"I-I-I'll have to give that some further study," he stuttered. "I'll get back to you."

I've been waiting since 1937 for him to get back to me. He never has. No, dear friend, when we're baptized in the Holy Ghost, the Spirit who gives us utterance to speak in other tongues is not a different spirit. He's the same Spirit who came into us when we were born again. This is just a different dimension of His work.

The New Birth is of utmost importance, but thank God for the baptism in the Holy Ghost and the enduement of heavenly power. I can remember ministering for three years without that experience, and I know there's a vast difference.

What the Scriptures Say

Let's begin with Jesus' own words concerning the work of the Spirit within and upon, and unfold through the Acts and the Epistles the glorious, continuing work of the Holy Spirit in the life of the believer.

Let's first look at four portions of Scripture. The first two are in the Gospel of John and the Acts of the Apostles.

JOHN 14:17
17 Even the Spirit of truth; whom the world cannot receive, because it seeth him not, neither knoweth him: but ye know him; for he dwelleth with you, and shall be IN you.

ACTS 1:8
8   But ye shall receive power, after that the Holy
Ghost is come UPON you: and ye shall be witnesses
unto me both in Jerusalem, and in all Judaea, and in
Samaria, and unto the uttermost part of the earth.

In the next scripture from chapter 4 of John's
Gospel, Jesus is speaking to the woman at the well of
Samaria.

JOHN 4:14
14   But whosoever drinketh of the water that I shall
give him shall never thirst; but the water that I shall
give him shall be IN him a well of water springing up
into everlasting life.

Now let's look in John chapter 7 at the fourth
portion of Scripture.

JOHN 7:37–39
37   In the last day, that great day of the feast, Jesus
stood and cried, saying, If any man thirst, let him
come unto me, and drink.
38   He that believeth on me, as the scripture hath
said, OUT OF HIS BELLY SHALL FLOW RIVERS
OF LIVING WATER.
39   (But this spake he of the Spirit, which they that
believe on him should receive: for the Holy Ghost was
not yet given; because that Jesus was not yet glorified.)

Notice from these four references that the Word of God speaks about both the Spirit *within* and the Spirit *upon*. I call this the dual working of the Holy Spirit. We can see from reading these verses, and others that we'll review, that it is quite evident there is a dual working of the Spirit of God. God expects this dual working of His Spirit in the lives of those who have accepted Jesus. As we look at this subject from the Bible, we'll see that there is also a twofold development God expects in His Spirit-filled children.

Water in the Well and Water in the River

In the first two scriptures, Christ promised the indwelling Spirit and also the outpouring of the Spirit. He promised the indwelling Spirit in John chapter 14: *"Even the Spirit of truth; whom the world cannot receive, because it seeth him not, neither knoweth him: but ye know him; for he dwelleth with you, and shall be IN YOU"* (v. 17). And Jesus promised the outpouring of the Spirit in Acts chapter 1: *"But ye shall receive power, after that the Holy Ghost is come UPON YOU. . ."* (v. 8). Jesus didn't say that we would be converted, or born again, when the Holy Ghost is come *upon* us. He said, *"But ye shall receive POWER . . . ,"* speaking of the subsequent experience of the Holy Spirit, the Holy Spirit upon.

Then in the last two scriptures from John's Gospel, we again see the twofold reference to the Spirit within and upon. Jesus said to the woman at the well of Samaria, *". . . whosoever drinketh of the water that I shall give him shall never thirst; but the water that I shall give him shall be in him a well of water springing up into everlasting life"* (John 4:14).

In the Scriptures, water is one of the types, or symbols, of the Holy Ghost. Jesus said, *". . . the water that I shall give him shall be IN HIM . . . ."* Notice that sounds a lot like what Jesus said about the Holy Ghost in John 14:17: *". . . he dwelleth with you, and shall be IN YOU."* And, talking about the Holy Spirit as water, Jesus said that water shall be *". . . a WELL of water springing up into everlasting life"* (John 4:14).

John chapter 4 refers to "water in the well," or the Spirit *within*. But Jesus also referred to the Holy Spirit as water in John chapter 7. This "water" refers to "water in the river," or the Spirit *upon*.

JOHN 7:37–39
37 In the last day, that great day of the feast, Jesus stood and cried, saying, If any man thirst, let him come unto me, and drink.
38 He that believeth on me, as the scripture hath said, out of his belly shall FLOW RIVERS OF LIV-ING WATER.
39 (But this spake he of the Spirit, which they that believe on him should receive: for the Holy Ghost was not yet given; because that Jesus was not yet glorified.)

Now notice that in John 4:14, the reference is to an *inward* state: *". . . the water that I shall give him shall be IN HIM a well of water springing up into everlasting life,"* or eternal life. Here Jesus is talking about receiving eternal life. ("Everlasting life" and "eternal life" are identical.) John 4:14 refers to an inward state that benefits the one so blessedly indwelt.

But the second reference, John 7:37–39, makes provision for others to whom the blessings of the Spirit flow forth *from* the believer after he or she is baptized in the Holy Spirit. In the baptism with the Holy Spirit, the Spirit comes *upon* the believer. Although water in the well is for the believer's own individual benefit, Jesus talked in John 7:37–39 about rivers flowing out of those who believe on Him. Now water is in both wells and rivers, but the water in the river is used for a different purpose than the water in the well. That was especially true in Jesus' day.

So we can see that water is a type or symbol of the Holy Spirit. And we can see a *dual* or *twofold* working and experience in connection with the Spirit of God as "water."

Fruit and Gifts

Now it is rather significant that we have two groups of nine characteristics and gifts in connection with these two works of the Spirit. The first group is mentioned in Galatians chapter 5 as the ninefold fruit of the Spirit. These might be referred to as characteristics resulting from the Spirit *indwelling* the believer.

GALATIANS 5:22–23
22 But the fruit of the Spirit is LOVE, JOY, PEACE, LONGSUFFERING, GENTLENESS, GOODNESS, FAITH,
23 MEEKNESS, TEMPERANCE: against such there is no law.

Then there is a second group of nine gifts found in First Corinthians chapter 12. These often are referred to as the "gifts of the Spirit."

1 CORINTHIANS 12:7–11
7 But the manifestation of the Spirit is given to every man to profit withal.
8 For to one is given by the Spirit the WORD OF WISDOM; to another the WORD OF KNOWLEDGE by the same Spirit;
9 To another FAITH by the same Spirit; to another the GIFTS OF HEALING by the same Spirit;
10 To another the WORKING OF MIRACLES; to another PROPHECY; to another DISCERNING OF SPIRITS; to another DIVERS KINDS OF TONGUES; to another the INTERPRETATION OF TONGUES:
11 But all these worketh that one and the selfsame Spirit, dividing to every man severally as he will.

Also these gifts of the Holy Spirit are given *". . . to profit withal . . ."* (1 Cor. 12:7). In other words, the gifts of the Spirit are given so that believers can bless others.

So from these two passages of Scripture, we can easily conclude that *the indwelling of the Spirit is for fruit-bearing, and the outpouring of the Spirit is for service.*

CHAPTER TWO

THE SPIRIT WITHIN: THE HOLY SPIRIT IN THE NEW BIRTH |

Beginning with this chapter, we're going to deal with the Holy Ghost as He is involved in the New Birth. As we said earlier, the Word of God suggests a dual working of the Spirit of God in those who believe on the Lord Jesus Christ.

The Holy Spirit comes *within* the believer in the New Birth or as it is sometimes called, conversion, being born again, receiving remission of sins, receiving eternal life, or receiving Christ as Savior and Lord. But on the other side of that dual working, the Holy Spirit comes *upon* the believer when he or she is baptized in the Holy Ghost. That is an experience of the enduement of power.

Look again in John chapter 14 at another reference to the Holy Spirit within. Here He is mentioned as the Comforter.

JOHN 14:16
16 And I [Jesus] will pray the Father, and he shall give you another Comforter, that he may ABIDE WITH you for ever.

Here the Lord promises the disciples another Comforter, implying that He, Jesus—their present Comforter—

would be removed and that another would be sent. And the coming of the Holy Spirit fulfilled this promise. The Holy Spirit already was *with* them because He was with Jesus, and Jesus was with them. But once the Father sent the Holy Ghost to the disciples, He—the Holy Spirit— would be *in* them (v. 17).

JOHN 14:17
17 Even the Spirit of truth; whom the world cannot receive, because it seeth him not, neither knoweth him: but ye know him; for HE DWELLETH WITH YOU, and SHALL BE IN YOU.

The Spirit of Truth—the Comforter—indwells those who believe in Jesus. Remember the Bible says, " . . . *if any man have not the Spirit of Christ, he is none of his*" (Rom. 8:9). The Spirit of Christ is the Holy Spirit, or the Holy Ghost.

Jesus of Nazareth could not be *in* the disciples physically because He had a resurrected flesh-and-bone body—a body that you could feel and see. After His resurrection, when He appeared on one occasion to His disciples and they said, "It is a spirit!" Jesus said, ". . . *HANDLE ME, AND SEE; for a spirit hath not flesh and bones, as ye see me have*" (Luke 24:39). And remember that Peter, preaching to Cornelius' household and talking about Jesus, said that he and the other disciples " . . . *did eat and drink with him after he rose from the dead*" (Acts 10:41).

Then Jesus of Nazareth ascended on high. His disciples watched Him as He left them. He is seated at the right hand of the Father, where He ever liveth to make intercession for us (Heb. 7:25; 8:1).

But it's through the power of the Holy Ghost that He enters us. The Bible says it is *" . . . Christ IN you, the hope of glory"* (Col. 1:27). Thanks be unto God, He sent the Holy Ghost, the Spirit of Christ, and He *could* be in us!

The Spirit of Adoption

Now another way to refer to the indwelling Spirit is as the Spirit of adoption. Paul uses that term in Romans.

ROMANS 8:15
15 For ye have not received the spirit of bondage again to fear; BUT YE HAVE RECEIVED THE SPIRIT OF ADOPTION, whereby we cry, Abba, Father.

We see the same thought in Galatians chapter 4.

GALATIANS 4:4–6
4 But when the fulness of the time was come, God sent forth his Son, made of a woman, made under the law,
5 To redeem them that were under the law, THAT WE MIGHT RECEIVE THE ADOPTION OF SONS.
6 And because ye are sons, GOD HATH SENT FORTH THE SPIRIT OF HIS SON INTO YOUR HEARTS, crying, Abba, Father.

Now remember that Jesus said the Comforter—the Holy Spirit—shall be in us. Galatians 4:6, which says, *". . . God hath sent forth the Spirit of his Son . . . ,"* refers to the Holy Ghost, or the Holy Spirit. And for one who has the Holy Spirit within him, Paul says, *"The Spirit itself* [a better translation would be "the Spirit Himself"] *beareth witness with our spirit, that we are the children of God . . ."* (Rom. 8:16). These verses in Romans and Galatians, which speak of our being children of God, or sons of God, refer to the New Birth, not to the baptism in the Holy Ghost. In the New Birth, the Holy Spirit is in our spirits, bearing witness with our spirits that we are the children of God.

Ezekiel's Prophecy About Spiritual Water

Now, let's turn back to the Old Testament and look at a prophecy concerning aspects of this work of the Holy Spirit within.

EZEKIEL 36:25–27
25 Then will I sprinkle clean water upon you, and ye shall be clean: from all your filthiness, and from all your idols, will I cleanse you.
26 A new heart also will I give you, and a new spirit will I put within you: and I will take away the stony heart out of your flesh, and I will give you an heart of flesh.
27 AND I WILL PUT MY SPIRIT WITHIN YOU, and cause you to walk in my statutes, and ye shall keep my judgments [my words], and do them.

Now notice two verses from the Book of Hebrews.

HEBREWS 8:10
10 For this is the covenant that I will make with the house of Israel after those days, saith the Lord; I will put my laws into their mind, and write them in their hearts: and I will be to them a God, and they shall be to me a people.

HEBREWS 10:16
16 This is the covenant that I will make with them after those days, saith the Lord, I will put my laws into their hearts, and in their minds will I write them.

I want you to notice that three things are included in Ezekiel's promise or prophecy. Number one: cleansing by clean water. Notice the expression in Ezekiel 36:25: *"Then will I sprinkle clean water upon you, and ye shall be clean: from all your filthiness, and from all your idols, will I cleanse you."* What does "cleansing by clean water" mean?

Well, coming to the New Testament, we might call this "the washing of the water of regeneration." Let's look in Titus 3:5 and we'll see what He means: *"Not by works of righteousness which we have done, but according to his mercy he saved us, BY THE WASHING OF REGENERATION, and renewing of the Holy Ghost."*

Paul was talking here about salvation, wasn't he? *". . . According to his mercy he saved us . . . ."* And how did God save us? "*. . . By the washing of regeneration, and renewing of the Holy Ghost.*" We might refer to the cleansing by clean water in Ezekiel 36:25 as the washing of regeneration in Titus 3:5.

Ephesians 5:26 gives us further insight into what Ezekiel prophesied about. "*That he* [Jesus] *might sanctify and cleanse it* [the Church] *with the washing of water by the word.*"

Hallelujah! You see, Christ cleanses the Church with the washing of water by the Word. That's what Ezekiel prophesied about. We learn then that one who submits himself to the Word of God is cleansed by that Word.

Now let's stop there for a minute. Acts 8:14 says, "*Now when the apostles which were at Jerusalem heard that Samaria had received THE WORD OF GOD . . . .*" What happened? The Samaritans had received the washing of water by the Word. Remember that Jesus once told His disciples, "*Now ye are clean THROUGH THE WORD which I have spoken unto you*" (John 15:3). And Peter told the disciples at Jerusalem that the angel who appeared to Cornelius the centurion told him, "*. . . Send men to Joppa, and call for Simon, whose surname is Peter; WHO SHALL TELL THEE WORDS, whereby thou and all thy house shall be saved*" (Acts 11:13–14).

Do you see that Christ cleanses the Church with the washing of water by the Word? *We learn then that one who submits to the Word of God for salvation may be regarded as being sprinkled with clean water.*

"I thought it was the Blood of Jesus that washed away our sins," someone might say.

We wouldn't know a thing about the Blood if we didn't have the Word of God to tell us about it.

So the first thing included in Ezekiel's prophecy and promise in connection with the Spirit within is cleansing by clean water. Secondly, one's spiritual nature is changed. Thank God! Remember, *"A new heart also will I give you, and a new spirit will I put within you . . ."* (Ezek. 36:26). This is talking about the New Birth of our human spirit.

And then thirdly, God puts His own Spirit within us. In Ezekiel 36:27, God says, *"And I will put my spirit within YOU, and cause you to walk in my statutes, and ye shall keep my judgments, and do them."* Through God's Spirit within us, He causes us to walk in His statutes and keep His judgments, or Word.

Cooperating With the Indwelling Spirit

Now concerning the indwelling Spirit, I believe there are three key truths we must bear in mind if we are going to fully cooperate with the Holy Spirit.

Number one: *Constant renewals of the Spirit are necessary.*

Number two: *It's important to walk in the Spirit,* in order that He may keep us fully informed of the manner in which God would have us live.

Number three: *We should learn the way of the Spirit* so that we can trace God's guiding hand of love amidst all of the circumstances that we encounter in our daily walk with Him.

Number One:
Renewals of the Spirit

Let's look more closely at these, considering first renewals of the Spirit. In order for us to benefit in our daily lives from the Presence of the Holy Spirit within us, we must experience constant renewals of God's quickening power in our spirit by the Holy Spirit.

Why are renewals of our spirit so important? Second Corinthians 4:16 says, ". . . *though our outward man perish, yet the inward man is renewed day by day.*"

You see, our bodies are continually growing older. Of course, a person who is strong in faith can delay the physical aging process to a certain extent. However, none of us can totally prevent the body from growing older and eventually dying. But what happens to the inward man as our outward man is decaying or aging? The inward man ". . . *is renewed day by day.*"

How is the inward man renewed day by day? Initially, our human spirit is regenerated or recreated by the Holy Spirit in the New Birth (Titus 3:5). Since the New Birth is a work of the Holy Spirit, the daily renewal of our spirit will also come through the same Source—the Holy Spirit who dwells within us.

In Paul's prayer for the Ephesian believers, we can see that it is the work of the Holy Spirit that brings about the renewing or strengthening of our spirit day by day.

EPHESIANS 3:16
16 That he would grant you, according to the riches of his glory, to be strengthened with might by his Spirit in the inner man.

Paul said believers need to be renewed or strengthened with might by God's Spirit in the inner man.

You see, one infilling of the Holy Spirit isn't sufficient. *Daily* renewals of your spirit are essential in order to keep you strong spiritually. That is done as you continually stay filled up to overflowing with the Holy Spirit.

In Ephesians 5:18, Paul exhorts believers to stay filled with the Holy Spirit. (And these believers were both born again *and* baptized with the Holy Ghost.)

EPHESIANS 5:18–19
18 And be not drunk with wine, wherein is excess; but BE FILLED [literally, be being filled] WITH THE SPIRIT;
19 Speaking to yourselves in psalms and hymns and spiritual songs, singing and making melody in your heart to the Lord.

A buoyant spirit of joy and praise is a result of staying continually filled up with the Holy Spirit. Staying filled with the Holy Spirit not only strengthens or renews the *believer*, but the joyful spirit of praise it produces also attracts the *unbeliever* and makes him desire a similar experience.

I remember talking to one minister who had been saved as a young man as a result of watching the life of a believer who knew how to stay renewed and filled up with joy and the Holy Ghost.

When this minister was a young man during the Depression days, his father died. He was the oldest child, so he had to drop out of high school and take a menial job doing hard manual labor in order to provide for the rest of the family.

Complaining to himself that he had received a bad lot in life, the young man became sour on life. He hardly ever smiled and always acted grouchy toward other people.

This young man worked on a road-building crew. As the days passed, he began to notice one particular co-worker. Instead of being grumpy and negative, this other man was always singing and was full of joy.

One day the young man told his co-worker, "I just can't figure you out. You're no better off than I am. You have to work just as hard to support your family as I do. How in the world can you be so joyful all the time? How can you always have a song to sing?"

The negative young man continued, "I don't have *anything* to be joyful about. I go to bed at night saying, 'I just wish my life would end so I wouldn't have to wake up in the morning.' I wake up every morning groaning about another day to live through. How can *you* be so joyful?"

The co-worker replied, "It's all because of Jesus! I've been born again, and that's why I can be so joyful."

Then he asked, "Why don't you go to church with me Sunday?"

The young man replied, "I will if you think it will do any good. I just want the same spirit of joy you have."

"Well, church is one place you can get it!" the co-worker exclaimed.

In relating his story, this man who later became a minister told me, "I went to church with this Christian man, and I found that all the other people in the church were full of joy too! I knew most of those people faced the same kind of difficult circumstances I faced. But they were happy and joyful, not bitter and negative like I was.

"I decided I was going to receive what those people had," this man concluded. "So I marched down to the altar and accepted Jesus!"

What made that man want to get saved? He was attracted to those believers because they were filled with joy and praise. They knew how to keep their spirit strong and renewed by the Holy Spirit!

You see, our joy isn't based on circumstances. Our joy is based on *Jesus*! We can continually maintain that buoyant spirit of joy and praise by focusing our attention on Him and by allowing His Spirit to renew our spirit day by day.

However, the renewing of your inner man doesn't just happen automatically. And it doesn't just happen because the Bible talks about it. *You* have a part to play. You must *seek God* in His Word and in prayer. As you do, the following verse promises that the Holy Spirit will renew and strengthen your spirit.

ISAIAH 40:31

31 But they that wait upon the Lord shall renew their strength; they shall mount up with wings as eagles; they shall run, and not be weary; and they shall walk, and not faint.

The phrase "wait upon the Lord" in this verse means *to be bound or entwined together* with the Lord; *to expect or to look patiently* for Him. It doesn't mean we should passively wait for God to renew our strength or renew our spirit. Rather, we are to bind ourselves closely to Him and His Word in intimate fellowship. As we diligently seek God, He will perform His Word on our behalf.

Sometimes folks think, *I'm walking by faith and maintaining my confession of God's Word. That's all that's necessary to keep my spirit strong and renewed.* Thank God for the Word that He has given us to strengthen us! But as important as the Word is in the daily renewal of our spirit, it can never take the place of waiting before the Lord in prayer. We need both prayer *and* the Word.

You know, there was much blessing and truth to the old-time Pentecostal tarrying meetings. Many of those Pentecostals experienced marvelous times in the Lord as they tarried or waited before God in prayer and praise. However, many other believers missed it by tarrying for the baptism of the Holy Spirit. But they didn't need to tarry for the infilling of the Holy Spirit, because that biblical experience already belonged to them as believers (Acts 2:39).

Believers don't have to tarry to receive the baptism of the Holy Spirit. They just need to receive that supernatural experience by faith as part of their rightful inheritance in Christ. Once believers are filled with the Holy Spirit, however, they should start tarrying or waiting before the Lord in prayer so their spirit can be renewed or strengthened by the Holy Spirit day by day!

Isaiah 40:31 is talking about the renewal of one's spiritual strength. However, I thoroughly believe that as a person is renewed and strengthened spiritually, it will also affect every part of his being—spirit, soul, and body.

For instance, daily renewals of your spirit by the Holy Spirit and the Word will positively affect your mind, which is part of your soul. We see the word "renew" used in reference to the mind in the Book of Romans.

ROMANS 12:2
2   And be not conformed to this world: but be ye transformed by the renewing of your mind, that ye may prove what is that good, and acceptable, and perfect, will of God.

Certainly it's true that your mind is renewed with the Word of God. But you don't get a renewed mind just because you memorize scriptures and make all the right confessions. No, that's only a part of it. Renewing the mind is a continual process. The Holy Spirit is involved in the renewing of your mind as you study and meditate on the Word (John 16:13).

As your spirit is renewed day by day, it will also affect your body. The Bible says that as you seek God, He will renew your youth as the eagle's.

PSALM 103:2,5
2   Bless the Lord, O my soul, and forget not all his benefits . . .
5   Who satisfieth thy mouth with good things; so that thy youth is renewed like the eagle's.

Someone once told me that a person reaches his physical peak at age thirty-five, and after that his physical strength declines. That's what the *world* believes. But I didn't believe that then, and I don't believe it now!

Even though our bodies age or decay, God has promised to quicken our mortal bodies (Rom. 8:11). As our spirit is renewed by the Holy Spirit, it will affect our body and cause our youth to be renewed.

I've seen preachers who believed that they had to get weaker as they got older. Some of those preachers could hardly wait until they could retire. By the time some of them were fifty-five, you'd think they were one hundred by the way they acted!

I remember one minister who saw the truth of this verse in Isaiah when he was an older man. Actually, this man didn't even begin his ministry until he was almost sixty years old. He had his greatest ministry between the ages of sixty-three and eighty-two. At seventy-five, he was the leading evangelist of his Full Gospel denomination in his state.

You see, when this minister was a young man, he knew God was calling him to the ministry as an evangelist. But his wife wasn't willing to make the sacrifice necessary to be in the ministry, so he finally agreed to stay home on their farm with her and raise their family.

Years passed, and the time came when their children were grown and on their own. This man told his wife, "I have to obey the call of God on my life. If you want to go with me, fine. If you don't, then stay on the farm. I'll take care of you, but I have to obey God."

As this minister prepared to get back into the ministry, the devil told him, "Look at you! You're almost sixty years old. You can never regain the years of ministry you've lost. Your ministry is over!"

But then this man read God's promise in Psalm 103:5 that God would renew his youth like the eagle's. He didn't know what that verse meant, so he went to the library to read about eagles.

He found out that eagles live many years. But as an eagle grows older, his beak wears out. When that happens, the eagle will die, since he has to have a strong beak to catch prey for food.

But an old eagle doesn't give up and die! Instead, he goes off somewhere and finds a rock. He starts beating his worn-out old beak on that rock, and he doesn't stop until it falls off. Then he grows another one!

When this minister read that about eagles, he took hold of that truth for himself. He beat his "beak" off on the Rock of Ages and believed God to strengthen his inner man by the Holy Spirit and renew his youth like the eagle's! He went into the ministry, and twenty years later at eighty years old, he was *still* one of the leading evangelists for his denomination!

Jesus is coming soon. And He wants to reap a harvest of precious souls of the earth before He comes (James 5:7). There's a great move of God on the earth in these last days. And I'm going to stay right in the middle of that move as I believe God for constant renewals of my spirit, mind, and body!

You need to do that too. Don't go through life without receiving the benefits of the precious Holy Spirit's indwelling Presence. Wait before the Lord in the Word and in prayer long enough to allow Him to renew your spirit day by day. As you do, it will affect every part of your being—spirit, soul, *and* body. Then you can walk in the newness of God's abundant life!

CHAPTER THREE

$\mathcal{W}$ALKING IN THE SPIRIT |

We've looked at the first of three key truths for the Spirit-indwelt believer, which was: constant renewals of the Spirit are necessary. The second thing that must be kept in mind by one indwelt by the Holy Spirit is that he or she must walk in the Spirit. Paul wrote about walking in the Spirit when he wrote about godliness. He wrote the following to Timothy.

1 TIMOTHY 4:8
8   For bodily exercise profiteth little: but godliness is profitable unto ALL things, having promise of the life that NOW IS, AND of that which IS TO COME.

Many Christians are glad because of the hope they have of Heaven, and rightly so. Thank God for the life that is to come! But there is an earthly side to life—a life that now is. In First Timothy 4:8, Paul deals with both the earthly and the heavenly sides of life. We need to be concerned about both of them. Yet it seems that some people are concerned about just one or the other.

We've heard it said for years that some people become so heavenly minded that they're no earthly good. It's all right to be heavenly minded. Just don't push it to the extreme.

On the other hand, some people become so *earthly* minded that they're no *heavenly* good. They are concerned only about the earthly side of life. But we can see from First Timothy 4:8 that God is interested in both the earthly and the heavenly sides of life. Godliness has "*. . . promise of the life that NOW IS, and of that which IS TO COME.*"

We can see that truth in Psalm 103. We often use several of these verses in preaching and teaching on healing, and we should!

PSALM 103:1–3
1   Bless the Lord, O my soul: and all that is within me, bless his holy name.
2   Bless the Lord, O my soul, and forget not all his benefits:
3   Who forgiveth all thine iniquities; who healeth all thy diseases . . . .

Thank God He forgives us *and* heals us. But that's not all the psalmist said. Look at the next two verses.

PSALM 103:4–5
4   Who redeemeth thy life from destruction; who crowneth thee with lovingkindness and tender mercies;
5   Who satisfieth thy mouth with good things; so that thy youth is renewed like the eagle's.

In verse 4, "redeemeth" means *saves*. Here the psalmist blesses God for redeeming, or saving, his earthly life from destruction. And under the New Covenant, that benefit belongs to us also (Heb. 8:6).

Now consider this carefully: *In order for us to enjoy such exemption from harm, God has given us His Spirit to sanctify or separate us from things that would destroy our peace or injure our health.* To walk in the Spirit is to walk in godliness.

We thank God for giving us His holy written Word. But did you ever stop to think that for most of the last two thousand years, Christians didn't have the Word to read? The letters written by Paul were read aloud to them at their gatherings. They didn't have anything to take home. There were no printing presses. They had to depend more upon the Spirit of God than we do.

Today, thank God, we have the written Word. Because we have it, we ought to be much further advanced spiritually than our brothers and sisters in Christ were through the centuries. But if we're not careful, dear friend, we'll focus exclusively on the Word of God and overlook the promptings of the Spirit. It's entirely possible to forget about the Spirit of God who dwells within us and have just a head knowledge of the Bible. Remember, though, ". . . *the letter killeth, but the spirit giveth life*" (2 Cor. 3:6). We need to learn to walk in the Spirit in order to have that life.

God said of the New Birth through Ezekiel's prophecy, "*And I will put my spirit within you, and cause you to walk in my statutes, and ye shall keep my judgments, and do them"* (Ezek. 36:27). In other words God said, "My Spirit within you will cause you to walk in and keep My Word."

Now don't misunderstand me. It's necessary to know the Word. But I have found in my own experience through the years that even when I didn't know the Word in particular cases, the Spirit of God led me in line with the Word, because I learned to follow the Spirit. I didn't know sometimes until years later when I found certain scriptures that the Spirit of God had led me in line with those verses. When I found them, I said, "Praise God, I knew the Spirit of God was leading me, but now here I see the Word on it!"

Psalm 103:4 says the Lord *". . . redeemeth* [or saveth] *thy life from destruction . . . ."* As I said, in order for us to enjoy such exemption from harm, God has given us His Spirit to sanctify or separate us from things that would destroy our peace, injure our health, or cause us to be destroyed.

Don't Ignore the Holy Spirit's Leading

A minister friend for whom I have preached a number of meetings was pastor of a church in Texas. Then he moved to California to pastor a church, and I preached meetings for him there. Now, I know this man. I spent time with him. He was a very outstanding man of faith who had many healings in his church. I don't think I was ever in any church where I saw more people healed than in the churches he pastored.

Well, while pastoring in California, he and his wife took a vacation and drove back to Texas to visit their families. Because this was a number of years ago, the interstate highway system wasn't complete. Travel times were usually longer than today.

The couple stopped overnight in Albuquerque, New Mexico, and continued on to Texas the next morning. Just east of Albuquerque, the two-lane road wound through mountains. It had been raining and was very slick. Coming around a curve, their car skidded. He braked but couldn't stop, and ran right into another car.

There already were two or three automobiles piled up, and two or three more crashed into their car from behind. A woman in the car their vehicle hit was killed, the minister's wife was critically injured, and their car was completely demolished. Because the minister and his wife believed God for the wife's healing, she was raised up by the power of God that very day and they were able to continue their journey.

Some time later, this minister had another severe automobile accident. He subsequently moved back to Texas to pastor, and I was in his church teaching about being led by the Spirit of God.[1] Afterward, he related the following story to me.

This minister told me that the morning of the first accident, he and his wife had gotten up, read from the Bible, and prayed. Then while she finished packing, he went outside to check the car over. (Now notice this, because here is something we need to learn.) He told me, "It just seemed like something on the inside of me said, 'Wait here ten minutes.' I didn't pay a lot of attention to it. I just went inside and got the suitcases. When I put them in the car, it seemed like something inside me said again, 'Wait here ten minutes.'"

The minister went back to the room to see if his wife was ready. Then they came out. He had already checked them out of the hotel. He said, "As we got into the car, it seemed like something on the inside of me said the third time, 'Wait here ten minutes.'

"I said, 'I believe God. I confess that the Lord will take care of me. There's no use waiting here. We're in a hurry. We have to get to Texas!'" So they drove off, and shortly afterward were involved in that accident.

You see, confession and believing the Bible are right. But if the Spirit of God tells us something, we had better obey Him. He wants to redeem our lives from destruction!

Now if the Holy Spirit doesn't say anything, then we should just go ahead and hold fast to our confession. But if the Spirit of God says something to us on the inside and we choose to ignore it, we can hold fast to our confession of protection and exemption from harm all day long, but we'll get into trouble like that minister did.

That minister was a great man of faith. And thank God he didn't give up his faith even though he had the accident. His faith saved his wife's life. She was unconscious and the doctors thought she would be dead in a few minutes. They tried to convince this minister not to pray for her because they thought if she did regain consciousness she would be severely impaired mentally and physically for the rest of her life. But the minister prayed anyway, and within an hour, his wife was up and out of the hospital!

That minister was a man of faith. He believed God. But he should have listened to the Holy Spirit.

There's no use in pointing a finger at him. I've been in the same boat! I've gotten into trouble more than once financially by not listening to that inward prompting of the Holy Spirit. Oh, I made all the proper confessions and said all the right things. God wants to prosper us. I believe that, and I believed and confessed His Word concerning His desire to prosper me. But the Holy Spirit tried to help me in a specific instance and I wouldn't listen.

During the late 1940s, I didn't know as much about faith as I know now, but I did know something. While at the last church I pastored, I invested a few hundred dollars in what looked like a good deal. Something on the inside of me told me not to invest that money, but I did it anyway, and I lost it. And a few hundred dollars then would be like several thousand dollars now.

I learned some of the things I know by making mistakes. When you're hurting in a few places, you don't forget a lesson so easily! If I can get you to learn to listen to the Holy Spirit inside you, you won't have to make some of the mistakes some of the rest of us have made.

Something on the inside of me told me not to invest that money. I don't mean some voice spoke like thunder out of Heaven! I didn't hear anything outwardly; I heard it in my spirit. We sometimes call it an *inward intuition*. At times it does seem like a voice speaks up. This particular time, it was more of an inward witness in my spirit saying, "Don't do that." But I let my head get in the way and didn't listen to that inward leading.

At the time, I was thinking of a lot of scriptures on prosperity, and one was "... *whatsoever he doeth shall prosper*" (Ps. 1:3). But we won't prosper when we walk in disobedience. We may say, "I see it in Scripture, so this plan will prosper. I'm going to claim it! The devil's not going to cheat me!" But a lot of times we haven't learned how to tell whether the devil or God is telling us to do something, or not to do it. Let's hold fast to our confession, but let's also learn to recognize the promptings of the Spirit of God and be sure we're listening to them!

Something inside told me not to invest that few hundred dollars back then in Texas. I know it just as well as I know my name. But I invested the money and lost it. And it took me a long time to get over it, because I had grieved the Spirit.

I did the same thing in a different way during the mid-1950s. I was finishing up a meeting in the First Foursquare Church in Long Beach, California, and was getting ready to go from there to the First Foursquare Church in Redondo Beach. I had already moved my travel trailer to a trailer park in Redondo Beach.

Now, different people have different makeups or traits. I'm a night person; I go to bed late. I'm usually more awake at midnight than at any other time. As a pastor, I did all my studying at night, because in the mornings, I usually wasn't as alert.

I'd go to bed anywhere from midnight to two a.m., so I didn't get up too early the next morning. In fact, when I had a ten a.m. teaching service, I'd get up just in time to get to it. I didn't want to clutter my mind with other things or get busy with anything else. I wanted my mind on my Bible lesson.

So one particular night, we had gone to bed late. Now, a number of times through the years, no matter how late I'd gone to bed, just as the sun came up, I'd sit straight up in bed out of a deep sleep. That's what happened that morning. I know, because the way our bed was situated, our heads were to the west and our feet to the east.

I suddenly sat straight up in bed. I could see the sun just beginning to rise. And I heard something. I knew it wasn't audible, but it seemed almost audible, like a voice speaking to me. It said, "There is a recession coming—not a depression, but a recession. Get ready for it." This was in May of 1956.

Well, I didn't listen. And not only did the Spirit of God speak to me that time, but I had another supernatural experience about two months later, and I let that get by me too. The recession came in 1957, and I went one hundred dollars in the red every single month for twelve solid months.

I'm not talking about not having extra money. I mean, we budgeted just barely enough to get along on and still were falling a hundred dollars a month short of that.

Thank God for life insurance. All I had to borrow money on were my life insurance policies. Now, I didn't buy life insurance policies because I thought I was going to die young. I knew I wasn't. I bought *endowment* policies. You see, with my meager income, I didn't save. I should have disciplined myself, but I didn't. There were too many other places for that money to go.

So I had purchased endowment policies that would pay themselves out in twenty years, and they were all paid out. I had four policies all together. That was my way of saving. Well, I had to go to the bank to borrow money, and I had no other collateral so I took those insurance policies because their cash value was high. I borrowed money to keep going. It was either that or do without or perhaps even quit.

And I prayed! You talk about a fellow praying! As we say, speaking in the natural vernacular, I prayed up a storm! God blessed me in other areas. I'd lay hands on the sick and they'd be healed. I'd lay hands on believers and they'd be filled with the Holy Ghost. People were saved. Gifts of the Spirit operated. But the Lord wouldn't say one word to me about my finances. Nothing. I had grieved the Spirit. I toughed it out for a solid year, and it was rough!

Well, on the last Sunday in December of 1957, I started a meeting in Port Neches, Texas, east of Houston, and we continued into 1958. A whole year had come and gone and the Lord hadn't said anything to me about my finances.

I'd gone back to the bank several times and borrowed more money. I hadn't even made any interest payments, and, finally, I went in to talk to the banker. He said, "We don't care whether you pay it now or not. If something happens to you, we'll get our money. After all, we're in the money-loaning business, and your insurance policies are good collateral."

Back in 1950, the Lord had dealt with me about prosperity and finances, and I had put all of those laws in motion and made all my confessions. But during 1957, I just went the whole year the opposite way, deeper into debt.

Well, early in 1958 we were still in the meeting in Texas, and one night a spirit of intercession suddenly fell upon us. I had nearly finished my message. I didn't have to ask anyone to pray. Everyone just hit the floor. They either came down to the front around the altar or stayed at or near their seats. I was still standing at the pulpit, and looked back across that church auditorium, and everyone was kneeling. No one was sitting on a pew.

I knelt down by a chair on the platform and began to pray. There was a real spirit of prayer present. We must have prayed anywhere from 45 minutes to an hour and 15 minutes. Finally, I got up and just sat down in the chair. Some folks were still at the altar praying. Others had gotten up and were sitting on pews.

As I sat there on that chair, singing in other tongues, suddenly, right in front of me, in plain sight, there stood Jesus. He talked to me about several things, including my ministry. Then finally He got down to his last subject. He began, "Now, about your finances . . ."

Whew! I was glad He brought that up! "Yes, Lord?" I said.

He continued, "You know that I spoke to you by My Spirit, and I saw you weren't going to listen. So when you were in California, I sent my angel down and he came into your trailer home. But you wouldn't listen, so I left you alone. I just let you suffer it out for a year."

"It's sure been tough too," I said.

Then He began to tell me how He was going to turn our finances around. He told me what would happen within a three-month period, and it happened just exactly as He said. I was so glad to get out of that financial bind!

Well, as I said, God has given us His Spirit to make it possible for us to enjoy exemption from anything that would injure or destroy our peace, health, or well-being. To be instructed and reminded by the indwelling Spirit is indeed a fine provision of our Heavenly Father. He wants to redeem our lives from destruction. But in order to consistently walk in the Spirit, we must learn to recognize and heed the Spirit's promptings.

---

[1] For more information on this subject, see Rev. Kenneth E. Hagin's book *How You Can Be Led by the Spirit of God.*

CHAPTER FOUR

THE IMPORTANCE OF WALKING IN LOVE |

We are establishing that there is a twofold work of the Spirit of God that God expects in the lives of Christians: the Holy Spirit *within* the believer, and the Holy Spirit *upon* the believer.

We also pointed out that the Spirit *within* the believer blesses the individual (John 4:14), and the Spirit *upon* the believer, the baptism with the Holy Spirit, produces blessings flowing out to others (John 7:38).

So the Holy Spirit comes *within* us at the New Birth for our own individual benefit. But the Holy Spirit comes *upon* us in the baptism of the Holy Ghost for service and witnessing (Luke 24:49; Acts 1:8).

In connection with the Holy Ghost *within* us, there are nine fruit of the Spirit mentioned in Galatians chapter 5, verses 22 and 23. And in connection with the Holy Ghost *upon* us, there are nine manifestations, or gifts, of the Holy Ghost listed in First Corinthians chapter 12, verses 7 through 11. Sometimes we emphasize certain parts of these truths, but they *all* should be emphasized because they're all important.

In conjunction with the Holy Ghost coming to dwell *within* us in the New Birth, we saw that three things are necessary for cooperating fully with the Holy Spirit within:

1. Constant renewals of the Spirit, accomplished by praying to and fellowshipping with the Father, and feeding on the Word of God.

2. Walking in the Spirit.

3. Learning the way of the Spirit.

Let's continue discussing walking in the Spirit by reviewing Galatians chapter 5. The Spirit of the Lord, or the Holy Ghost, said these things through the Apostle Paul. (Remember that Paul didn't write this letter to just one church, but to *all* churches in the region of Galatia to be read in each church.)

GALATIANS 5:16

16 This I say then, Walk in the Spirit, and ye shall not fulfil the lust of the flesh.

Often when we talk about walking in the Spirit, people become misty-eyed and foggy-headed. Some people think walking in the Spirit means that we just sort of float around with our head in the clouds. But walking in the Spirit is very simple and practical.

GALATIANS 5:17–19

17 For the flesh lusteth against the Spirit, and the Spirit against the flesh: and these are contrary the one to the other: so that ye cannot do the things that ye would.

18 But if ye be led of the Spirit, ye are not under the law.

19 Now the works of the flesh are manifest . . . .

To put it simply, this phrase could read, "If you are walking in the flesh, the flesh is dominating you, and this is the result."

GALATIANS 5:19–22
19 Now the works of the flesh are manifest, WHICH ARE THESE; Adultery, fornication, uncleanness, lasciviousness,
20 Idolatry, witchcraft, hatred, variance, emulations, wrath, strife, seditions, heresies,
21 Envyings, murders, drunkenness, revellings, and such like: of the which I tell you before, as I have also told you in time past, that they which do such things shall not inherit the kingdom of God.
22 But the fruit of the Spirit is . . . .

We wouldn't be changing the meaning if we were to begin verse 22 with the phrase, "But to walk in the Spirit is to walk in . . . ."

GALATIANS 5:22–23
22 But the fruit of the Spirit is love, joy, peace, longsuffering, gentleness, goodness, faith,
23 Meekness, temperance: against such there is no law.

So to walk in the Spirit is to walk in love, joy, peace, longsuffering, gentleness, goodness, faith, meekness, and temperance. And against such, there is no law.

In verse 25 Paul says, *"If we live in the Spirit, let us also walk in the Spirit."* To walk in the Spirit is to walk in these nine fruit of the Spirit. That simplifies it, doesn't it?

Of these ninefold fruit of the Spirit, the very first one is *love*. We've already established that this fruit of the Spirit is produced by the Holy Spirit—the Spirit of Christ, or the life of Christ—within us. Fruit grows on the branch. Jesus said, *"I am the vine, ye are the branches . . ."* (John 15:5). So you see, we are the branches where the fruit grows.

We've established that the very first fruit of the recreated, born-again human spirit is love, because of the life of Christ within a person in the power and Person of the Holy Ghost. John said in his first Epistle, *"We know that we have passed from death unto life, because we love . . ."* (1 John 3:14). If we don't love, we don't have any evidence of salvation, of having passed from death unto life. Love is the very first fruit that will show up when we are born again!

I pointed out previously that this was one of the things in my own life that changed drastically when I was born again. Our home had been broken up because my father had left, and I was physically handicapped. People told me that I was mad at everyone. I hated the whole world. But when I was born again and the love of God was shed abroad in my heart, I loved everyone. It made such a difference.

But I have a choice as to whether or not I will let that love dominate me. In other words, I don't have to let that love dominate me. That love is in my heart, but if my mind isn't sufficiently renewed with the Word of God, my mind will side in with my flesh and derail me, so to speak. I would be a babe in Christ, a carnal Christian. Paul called the Corinthians carnal, baby Christians because there was strife among them (see 1 Cor. 3:1).

Because the Corinthian Church was walking in the flesh, there was strife, division, and debate among them. Paul told them, "You're babes," and, "You walk as mere men" (1 Cor. 3:1–3). In other words, Paul said, "you're walking like people who are not even saved when you let these things dominate you."

So, it's possible for a Christian to not allow the love of God to dominate him. But if he wants to be a successful Christian, he must let it dominate him. He needs to realize that it is up to him to do something with this love.

Now we pointed out that Romans 5:5 says, "*. . . the love of God is shed abroad in our hearts by the Holy Ghost . . . .*" It's in there! But what have we done with it? Have we put it into action, into practice? Or are we like the fellow with the one talent in Jesus' parable? Instead of putting that talent to use, he just wrapped it up in a napkin and hid it (Matt. 25:24–25; Luke 19:20). No, we need to let the love of God out, praise God!

Walking in Love Leads to Divine Health

Another important aspect of walking in love has to do with divine healing!

I use the following illustration quite frequently. I was holding a meeting in the western part of the nation, and in the meeting were a young man and his wife. They had three children. One was their natural child and two were adopted.

The last child they adopted was in perfect health until age two, when she began to have epileptic seizures. The parents took her to the most renowned specialist in that area of medicine in the Western Hemisphere. After that doctor ran tests on the child, he said, "This is the worst case I've seen in all of my years of practice."

Well, this couple was endeavoring to stand on the promises of God and accept healing for that child. But as I talked with this woman, she said to me, "I hate my mother-in-law. And the way you preach, I don't even know if I'm saved."

I said, "Well, if you really do hate your mother-in-law, you're not saved." John said in his first Epistle, *"Whosoever hateth his brother is a murderer: and ye know that no murderer hath eternal life abiding in him"* (1 John 3:15). And that means whoever hates *anyone*, not just his brother.

I knew that she was saved, but was only letting her flesh and human reasoning dominate her. So I said to her, "Look me right in the eye and say, 'I hate my mother-in-law.' And while you're saying that, look on the inside, in your spirit, and tell me what happens down there."

So she looked me in the eye and said, "I hate my mother-in-law." I said, "What happened down on the inside of you?"

She said, "There is something down there scratching me."

I said, "Yes. The Bible says, '. . . *the love of Christ constraineth us . . .* ' [2 Cor. 5:14]. The Holy Spirit is trying to get your attention."

"What am I going to do?" she said.

"Act as you would if you did love her, because you do. Let that love out!" I responded.

She invited my wife and I, her mother-in-law, and her sister-in-law over to their home for dinner. During the meal, she came around and whispered to me, "You're right. I don't hate my mother-in-law. I love her. They are very lovely people, and they love the Lord."

Later, this woman called the motel where my wife and I were staying, and my wife took the call. The woman said, "I know that Brother Hagin doesn't pray for everyone who asks. (With two meetings a day, I just didn't have time.) But would he consider coming and praying for our child?" Before a person goes into the main epileptic seizure, he goes into a preliminary attack, and this child was in that preliminary stage right then. The Spirit of God told me to go, so I told my wife, "Okay, we'll go!"

As we drove to this couple's house, the Lord spoke to me. My wife and I weren't saying anything to one another. We were being quiet, waiting on God. And just as if someone was sitting in the back seat of our car, the Holy Spirit said to me, "Don't pray for that child. Don't lay your hands on her. Don't touch her. Don't anoint her with oil. Don't minister to the child.

"Say to the mother, 'In the Old Testament I said to Israel, "Walk in My statutes and keep My commandments, do that which is right in My sight and I'll take sickness away from the midst of you, and the number of your days I will fulfill."'"

Then the Holy Spirit said, "Paraphrasing that in New Testament language, I said to the Church and to My disciples, 'I give you a new commandment, that you love one another. By this shall all men know that you are My disciples, because you have love one toward another'" (John 13:34–35; Gal. 5:14).

Of course, I knew what God said under the Old Covenant in Exodus chapter 23.

EXODUS 23:25–26
25 And ye shall serve the Lord your God, and he shall bless thy bread, and thy water; and I WILL TAKE SICKNESS AWAY FROM THE MIDST OF THEE.
26 There shall nothing cast their young, nor be barren, in thy land: THE NUMBER OF THY DAYS I WILL FULFIL.

We could translate these verses this way and do them no injustice: "Keep My commandment of love, and I will take sickness away from the midst of you, and the number of your days I will fulfill."

Then the Holy Spirit said, "Say to that mother, 'Tell Satan, "Satan, I'm walking in love now. Take your hands off my child."'"

We arrived at this couple's house, and when I said that to the mother, she didn't hesitate for a moment. She said right out loud, "Satan, I'm walking in love now. Take your hands off my daughter!" As fast as you can snap your fingers, that epileptic seizure stopped.

I saw the couple several years later and asked them if their daughter had ever had another attack. They said she never had. The mother said that a couple of times it seemed a few little symptoms would start to appear. I asked her what she did. She said, "I just said, 'Satan, I'm walking in love.'"

Now if we're not walking in love, we can't do that. But we need to begin walking in love. Walking in love is walking in the Spirit. It doesn't take long to jump over into walking in love. We need to ask the Lord to forgive us for not doing it, and declare, "From this moment on, I'm walking in love." Then we're in a position to start doing what this mother did.

If we could just get this over to everyone, we'd have to go outside the church to find someone to pray for, because there wouldn't be anyone inside the church to minister to! Someone might say, "I wish that would work for me." It doesn't work by wishing; it works by *doing* it!

Now Romans 5:5 says the love of God is shed abroad in our hearts. Therefore, the God-kind of love has been shed abroad in our hearts. The love of God is the God-kind of love. It's divine love, not natural, human love. If you've ever had any experience with natural, human love, you know that it is very selfish. But divine love is unselfish.

I particularly like the way *The Amplified Bible* words First Corinthians chapter 13:4–8. It is to be regretted that, in referring to this divine love, the translators of the *King James Version* rendered it "charity." Perhaps at that time, and to them, it meant that. But actually the Greek word *agape*, which means "love," is the same word used in Romans 5:5: "*. . . the LOVE of God is shed abroad in our hearts by the Holy Ghost . . . .*"

Following is the *King James* translation of First Corinthians 13:4–8.

1 CORINTHIANS 13:4–8

4 Charity suffereth long, and is kind; charity envieth not; charity vaunteth not itself, is not puffed up,

5 Doth not behave itself unseemly, seeketh not her own, is not easily provoked, thinketh no evil;

6 Rejoiceth not in iniquity, but rejoiceth in the truth;

7 Beareth all things, believeth all things, hopeth all things, endureth all things.

8 Charity never faileth: but whether there be prophecies, they shall fail; whether there be tongues, they shall cease; whether there be knowledge, it shall vanish away.

Now let's look at these verses in *The Amplified Bible.* It would help most Christians if we'd just read these verses every day for about six months. Then they would get down inside of us, and we would start practicing them.

> 1 CORINTHIANS 13:4–8 (*Amplified*)
> 4 Love endures long and is patient and kind; love never is envious nor boils over with jealousy, is not boastful or vainglorious, does not display itself haughtily.
> 5 It is not conceited (arrogant and inflated with pride); it is not rude (unmannerly) and does not act unbecomingly. Love (God's love in us) does not insist on its own rights or its own way, for it is not self-seeking; it is not touchy or fretful or resentful; it takes no account of the evil done to it [it pays no attention to a suffered wrong].
> 6 It does not rejoice at injustice and unrighteous-ness, but rejoices when right and truth prevail.
> 7 Love bears up under anything and everything that comes, is ever ready to believe the best of every person, its hopes are fadeless under all circumstances, and it endures everything [without weakening].
> 8 Love never fails [never fades out or becomes obsolete or comes to an end] . . . .

Let's look more closely at some of these verses. "Love endures long and is patient and kind . . ." (v. 4). A lot of people endure long just because they have to, but they're not patient and kind while they do it. They just suffer because they must.

"... Love never is envious nor boils over with jealousy ..." (v. 4). Natural, human love is jealous. But this God-kind of love doesn't boil over with jealousy.

"... Love (God's love in us) does not insist on its own rights or its own way, for it is not self-seeking ..." (v. 5).

I wish we would take time for that to soak in. "Love is not self-seeking" means that divine love is not selfish. In natural affairs, instead of walking in the Spirit and walking in love, Christian people often say, "I know what's mine. I'm going to have my say-so. I'm going to have my rights, no matter how much it might hurt someone else!" But this verse says, "Love does not insist on its own rights."

We'll never make it until we start believing in God—until we start believing in love. Love is the best way! Love is God's way, and love is *our* way!

I know something from having walked with the Lord for more than sixty-five years. Thank God, He has enabled me to walk in health. Living a healthy life doesn't just belong to me; it belongs to every believer. But to walk in health, we have to walk in love.

I tell people quite frequently that I haven't had a headache since August of 1933, so it's too late to start having headaches now, praise God! But some folks get angry with me for saying that. They don't understand what I mean.

Don't misunderstand me. You might have *opportunities* to have a headache. But you don't have to accept a headache. You can pass up those opportunities to have a headache or to be sick. Now, it's not wrong to have a headache, but it's wrong to keep it. You ought to get rid of it. But in order to receive healing and walk in health, we must be very careful to walk in love.

Love Does Not Insist On Its Own Rights

A number of years ago, my wife and I were finishing up a meeting in a Full-Gospel church when we were asked to change our plans. We were to begin a meeting at another church in that state. But the pastors of the church where we were, and the one we were to go to, along with several other pastors from that same denomination, asked us to delay our scheduled meeting for a week to hold services in a neighboring church of that same denomination.

So on Sunday night, we closed out the current meeting. I had received just enough money during that meeting to pay my bills. The next day, I used a credit card to buy gasoline and we headed over to the other church where we were to start the new meeting Monday night. I didn't have any cash with me. *Surely they'll provide our meals*, I thought.

Well, we arrived late because we had to drive some distance to get there. We were to stay at the parsonage with the pastor and his wife. When we got there, they never said anything about eating. I thought nothing of it. I often don't like to eat before I go to church anyway. *We'll eat afterwards,* I thought.

But after the first meeting, the pastor and his wife said nothing about going out and getting anything to eat. We drove back to the parsonage, and they didn't say anything about eating then either. They just went to bed, so we did too.

Now during that particular meeting, we had only night services. The next morning, the pastor and his wife got up before we did, and left. I thought maybe they'd been called to the hospital or had some other emergency—the phone had rung a time or two. I told my wife, "They'll probably be back soon and we'll go out to eat." But by 1:30 p.m., they hadn't shown up.

Well, we hadn't had anything to eat since we left that other church on Sunday, and it was now Tuesday at 1:30 in the afternoon. I told my wife, "Go into the kitchen and see if you can find anything to eat. They're not here, and they didn't say anything about eating." She came back and said, "I found one hot dog, two eggs, and one slice of bread." I told her to boil the eggs, and we each ate a boiled egg, half a slice of bread, and half a hot dog. That's all we could find.

"That'll tide us over until tonight," I said. "They'll probably come in early and take us out to the cafeteria or somewhere else to eat." I didn't want to eat before service, but I'd go anyway, because I was getting a little hungry! That egg and half a piece of bread and half a hot dog didn't last long!

Well, the pastor and his wife came in, but they didn't say anything about eating. They just got ready for church and left. And after the service, they just came home and went to bed. Wednesday morning, they got up and left before breakfast, and didn't fix any food, and they had nothing in their refrigerator. We knew that, because we'd eaten the last food they had. So from Sunday to Wednesday my wife and I had each eaten one boiled egg, half a slice of bread, and half of a hot dog—and several glasses of water!

Well, I thought maybe they'd be back at noon. But by 1:30 in the afternoon, they hadn't returned. So, instead of walking in the Spirit, I got over into the flesh. That's easily done, because we're already living in the flesh.

"What kind of people are these anyhow?" I asked my wife. "I know what I'll do. I know the district superintendent. I'll just call him and ask him, 'What kind of preachers do you have up here in your district?'" I knew the district superintendent well and I knew he'd get hold of them immediately and wring their necks for the way they'd been treating us.

So I went to the phone and started dialing the number. And then, right in the middle of dialing, something on the inside of me rose up. The love of Christ constrained me. I just hung up the phone.

"Well, aren't you going to phone?" asked my wife, who was standing nearby.

"No," I said, "I'm not going to phone. I don't want to get those dear people in trouble."

You see, it's true that we have our rights, but the Bible says that love doesn't insist on its own rights. It was right for that pastor and his wife to take care of us. They were obligated. But I wasn't going to get them into trouble for not doing it. Because of their behavior, they'd have enough trouble in life as it was, without my adding to it. People who treat others like that will have trouble. But I wasn't going to be responsible for their getting into trouble. I was going to walk in love.

Well, by the next day, we still hadn't had anything to eat, and I was ready to call the district superintendent again. My stomach got the upper hand. By then it was rubbing my backbone! I went to the phone, again ready to ask that superintendent, "What kind of people do you have in your district, anyway?" He was a personal friend of mine, and I'd never met these pastors before. I'd just tell him what happened, and I knew he'd call them on the carpet, so to speak.

I started to dial again—and even got a digit or two further than I did the day before. But then, before the phone started ringing, I hung up. "No," I said, "I'm not going to get them into trouble."

Just then one of the deacons, who lived about half a block away, knocked on the door. I answered it, and he introduced himself. I could see that he was concerned. He knew we'd been there all week and that the pastor and his wife had left early each day and hadn't come back until late.

"Brother Hagin, where are the pastors?" he asked.

"Oh," I said, "I'm sure they had an emergency call. I heard the phone ring a time or two."

He said, "I noticed that they leave about seven o'clock every morning. Have you and your wife had anything to eat?"

I didn't want to get the pastor in trouble, so I said, "We're doing all right."

"Well," he said, "I just felt led to come down and tell you that I live nearby." He took me out to the front porch and pointed out his house. "The back porch is screened in, and we have a freezer there," he said. "We keep the back door to the house locked, but the porch doors are open. Just go down there and get anything you'd like from the freezer if you want to cook something."

"Well, thank you," I said. "If they don't show up soon, we probably will." So we walked over to that deacon's house and got some food and had something to eat!

We stayed in that pastor's house all week, and he and his wife never said a word about eating anything, but from Thursday on, we got food from that freezer. I never said anything to anyone about it because I didn't want to get that pastor and his wife in trouble. I knew that if they kept walking that way, they'd get into trouble, anyway, without me adding to it.

I would rather let the Lord attend to the situation than get involved myself. When you're involved in getting someone else into trouble, you're going to get into trouble. Two wrongs don't make a right.

CHAPTER FIVE

LOVE IS THE BEST WAY

At the last church I pastored, the pastor who was there just before me had gotten into difficulty. I'm a preacher, and because I can appreciate the challenges of the ministry, I defend preachers. But preachers can be wrong too. They are as human as anyone else is.

This former pastor had been elected for a three-year period. If he had acted right during that time, no doubt he would have been reelected. But he didn't act right, so the church didn't reelect him.

The Lord spoke to me supernaturally to take the pastorate of that church, and later I understood why He did. But this former pastor stayed in the area and would visit members of the congregation who had supported him. He even held some meetings. I always knew when he did, and as I stepped behind the pulpit to preach on Sunday morning, I'd say to myself, *Brother So-and-so is back*. I could detect it in the congregation. I could tell that he'd been visiting those in the congregation who were on his side, telling them things and even collecting money from them.

I remember the regional director of the denomination of which this congregation was a part once said to me, "Brother Hagin, if you say so, we'll just take his papers away from him. We'll kick him out of the fellowship."

I said, "No, no! I'm not going to do it! The poor fellow is in trouble. I know he's wrong, but there's no use in ruining his ministry. I'm not going to do it. I'm going to act in love whether anyone else does or not."

Now this was just after World War II, and there weren't any wallpaper hangers in our area. I had done some paperhanging and painting through the years to supplement my income. This minister was building a new house and planned to sell it and move. He stopped by the parsonage and asked me if I knew anyone who did paperhanging. "No, there's no one around here," I said. "I've inquired about that myself. But I'll tell you what I'll do. I'll canvas and paper your house for you."

"Would you?" he asked.

"Sure I will," I said. And I did. When I finished, he and his wife came by and he asked me how much he owed me.

I said, "The Lord told me just to give that work to you."

Now I hadn't said a word to this minister or his wife, who was also a minister, about anything they had done, but both of them began to cry. They said, "Well now, we never have spoken against you."

I said, "I know you haven't. You didn't know anything to speak against me about! But dear brother, did you ever stop to think that when you visited some of the church members and told them they were out of the will of God, and that you ought to still be pastor, you created strife and division, and you might as well have been speaking against me?"

"I never have gotten any of your tithes," he said.

I mentioned certain families, and told him they hadn't given the church a dime in the several months I'd been there.

"Well, they did give me money," he said, "but they didn't tell me it was tithes."

I said, "That's all right. If they weren't going to put it into the church, I'd rather that you have it, anyway, and that it be used in the work of God somewhere. So don't bother about it."

When they had sold the new house they had built and were ready to leave the area, I told them, "Before you leave, you and your wife both come to the church and preach."

"Oh, no!" he said. "They don't like us up there."

I said, "I know better. People who voted against you like you! They told me they did. Now come on up and preach, both of you."

So they came. One of them preached in the morning, and the other preached in the evening. We had glorious services, and they left in love. And that's best.

When that former pastor preached in the evening service, he said, "Folks, I want to admit that I'm wrong." It takes a big man to do that.

He said, "I'm sorry to say that I visited some of you whom I thought were on my side, and I kept telling you that God couldn't bless this church because I ought to be the pastor. I didn't exactly say it, but I implied that you and Brother Hagin were out of the will of God because I ought to be leading the church. But I was wrong. God loves His sheep. He loves His people, and He sent you someone to shepherd you.

"As I look over the crowd, I see that the building is full. It was never full when I was pastor here. I want you to know, Brother Hagin, that I rejoice that the building is full, that you're reaching people, and that God is blessing you. And I'm for you. God bless you!" Everyone got blessed and started crying, and we just had a glorious time in the Lord.

Just as Paul wrote in First Corinthians 13:8, I believe that "Love never fails."

Love's Thermometer

In reviewing First Corinthians 13:5 in *The Amplified Bible*, we see that "Love . . . is not touchy or fretful or resentful; it takes no account of the evil done to it [it pays no attention to a suffered wrong]."

Sometimes we would rather hear something else, wouldn't we? But this verse is love's thermometer—love's *gauge*. It's easy to find out whether we're walking in love or whether we're walking in the Spirit.

When we take account of the evil done to us, we're not walking in love. As long as we walk in God, in the Spirit, or in love, and stay full of the Spirit, we won't take any account of the evil done to us.

Through the years, I've had other situations like those mentioned earlier happen to me in my ministry. And relatives, other ministers, and even neighboring pastors have told me, "I wouldn't take that if I were you. I wouldn't put up with that."

Some neighboring pastors even told me that I must have a weakness in my character because I wouldn't fight people who fought me. I wouldn't say anything bad about them. Instead, I'd pray for them, and if I got the chance, I'd do something good for them.

The Bible says, " . . . *Love your enemies, bless them that curse you, do good to them that hate you, and pray for them which despitefully use you, and perse-cute you*" (Matt. 5:44). Yet Full Gospel pastors sug-gested that I must have a weakness in my character because I wouldn't fight people who fought me. No, it was *strength* that I had, not weakness, because love never fails!

Many have failed, and even died prematurely, because they lived so much in the natural that they couldn't take advantage of the privileges and blessings that rightfully belonged to them as children of God. They were always fussing and fighting, and that had an effect upon them, not only spiritually, but also physically.

Judging Ourselves

Christians should read and heed First Corinthians chapter 11. In that chapter, Paul said, *"For this cause many are weak and sickly among you, and many sleep"* (v. 30). Believers in Corinth were dying prema-turely because of their behavior. He continued, *"For if we would judge ourselves, we should not be judged.*

But when we are judged, we are chastened of the Lord, that we should not be condemned with the world" (vv. 31–32).

This biblical principal should be taught in churches when the Lord's Supper is commemorated. Paul chastised the Corinthians for not walking in love toward one another when they came together as a church. There were cliques, and they were being selfish. They didn't recognize that each of their number was a part of the Body of Christ, and should be treated as such (see verses 18–22,29). In these verses, Paul is talking about walking in love.

I saw one of the foremost healing evangelists of the 1950s die young because he continually walked out of love.

From 1947 through 1958, there was a healing revival in America. About 120 of us in the healing ministry belonged to an organization of evangelists called The Voice of Healing. We held conventions, and Gordon Lindsay published many of the healing testimonies in his magazine, *The Voice of Healing.*

The leading healing evangelist of that time had a tent that seated 20,000 people. One fellow in The Voice of Healing organization got an even larger tent by adding another section so he could seat 22,000. Occasionally, he'd fill up the tent.

The minister with the bigger tent was also one of the leading healing evangelists in the days of *The Voice of Healing.* No one had a greater healing ministry at that time than he did. I saw some of the greatest miracles in this evangelist's ministry that I'd ever seen.

During these days, the Spirit of God said to me, "You go tell [and He called this evangelist's full name] that he's not going to live much longer unless he judges himself." The man was only thirty-five years old at the time.

The Lord said to me, "The number one thing he's to judge himself on is walking in love toward his fellow ministers." (You see, it is possible for us to judge ourselves on whether or not we're walking in love.) If anyone happened to oppose this minister, he'd call his name publicly and "get after him tooth and toenail," as we say in Oklahoma.

I went to talk to this healing evangelist, but he was busy talking to someone else at the time. By the time he finished talking to the other person, my natural mind had taken over, and I thought, *He doesn't walk in love toward the brethren. If I tell him what the Lord told me, he's liable to slap my face.* By then the evangelist had left, and I never had another opportunity to talk to him.

Well, I'm sorry to say that this minister didn't judge himself on love or any of the other areas the Lord mentioned. And in three years' time, he was dead.

Before this evangelist died, the Lord reminded me of why his life had come to the end it had. In November of 1956, around Thanksgiving, as we were in Angelus Temple in Los Angeles holding our annual Voice of Healing convention, word came that this dear minister was stricken and at the point of death. So

Brother Gordon Lindsay asked all the ministers to
come to the front and pray for him.

Three years had passed since the Lord had spoken
to me about this man, and I had temporarily forgotten
what the Lord had said to me about him. I started
walking down the aisle toward the platform to join
hands with the other Voice of Healing ministers—we
had many of them—and pray for our dear brother.

Suddenly, the Spirit of God said to me, "Don't go
up there. Don't pray. He's going to die." I stopped and
asked, "Why, Lord? He's only thirty-eight years of age.
You promised us at least seventy or eighty years, or
until we're satisfied. If we're not satisfied at eighty, we
can go on to ninety. If we're not satisfied with ninety,
we can live on to 100. If we're not satisfied with 100,
we can go on from there. You said, '*With long life will
I satisfy him, and shew him my salvation*' [Ps. 91:16].
And thirty-eight years is not long life."

The Lord said to me, "He wouldn't judge himself
and walk in love toward his fellow ministers. So I
judged him and turned him over to Satan for the
destruction of the flesh, that his spirit may be saved in
the day of the Lord Jesus" (see First Corinthians 5:5).
When you look at the fifth and eleventh chapters of
First Corinthians, you'll see that. And this time, not
walking in love was the only area the Lord mentioned
in which that evangelist had needed to judge himself.

So I just turned around and walked back up the
aisle and let the other ministers pray. There was no use
in getting into a discussion at that time.

My wife had been in another part of the auditorium and came to meet me. "What did the Lord say to you?" she asked.

"How do you know He said anything?" I responded.

"You just stopped dead still and turned white as a sheet," she said. "I know the Lord said something to you."

"Well, He said, 'Don't pray. He's going to die,'" I told her. And, sure enough, he did.

That wasn't God's best for him, friend, and it didn't have to happen to him. *That evangelist* was responsible for what happened to him.

Someone who doesn't know the Bible might hear of that man's death and say, "See, healing doesn't work. Here's a fellow in the healing business who died at 38 years of age, so that proves that healing is not for everyone."

Well, I'd just as soon hear a donkey bray at midnight in a tin barn! That poor old donkey doesn't know any better! You'd think anyone who can read would know better than that. Healing belonged to that evangelist. But we have to realize that many of the provisions of God, including healing, are *conditional*.

For instance, God is the same under the New Covenant as He was under the Old Covenant. He didn't say to Israel, "I'm going to take sickness away from the midst of you, and the number of your days I'll fulfill" (Exod. 23:25,26), and just leave it at that. No! *There were conditions they had to meet.*

God said to the Israelites, *"Walk in My statutes and keep My commandments,* and I will take sickness away from the midst of you, and the number of your days I will fulfill" (Exod. 23:20–22; Lev. 26:3,14–15; Deut. 28:1,15).

When we come over into the New Testament, we find the same thing. To paraphrase the Old Testament conditions in New Testament language, we can say, "You walk in My commandment of love and keep My statute of love, and I'll take sickness away from the midst of you, and the number of your days I will fulfill."

That's what the Spirit told me to tell that evangelist. But he didn't walk in God's commandment of love, so the Lord didn't take sickness away from him, and the number of his days He did not fulfill.

Nothing Is So Beautiful

Notice First Corinthians 13:5 again in *The Amplified Bible,* ". . . It [love] takes no account of the evil done to it [it pays no attention to a suffered wrong]." That has to be the God-kind of love. The Bible says that we were not only sinners but also enemies of God (Rom. 5:10; Col. 1:21). And He didn't take any account of the evil we had done to Him. He sent Jesus to redeem us. He loved us while we were yet sinners (Rom. 5:8).

If we would walk in the God-kind of love and pay no attention to a suffered wrong, can you see how that would straighten things out in the home, the church, the nation, and everywhere else? For men to become children of God, have the love of God in them, live in the family of God as His children, and walk in love—nothing is so beautiful!

Love Can Do It

Continuing on in First Corinthians chapter 13, "It [love] does not rejoice at injustice and unrighteousness, but rejoices when right and truth prevail. Love bears up under anything and everything that comes . . ." (vv. 6–7 *Amplified*). Someone facing a seemingly impossible task may say, "I just can't do it." Some people say, "I just can't take it. I can't put up with it any longer!" But love can! The Bible says right here that it can. And the love of God is in us, so *we* can!

Think about God. He's putting up with *all* of us. I pastored for nearly twelve years, and sometimes it was difficult to put up with certain people. But sometimes at night I would think about situations and start laughing. I'd say, "My, my! I'm about to get impatient with just a few people, and God is putting up with *all* of us!"

"Yes, but He's God!" someone might say.

I know it. But the Bible says we're made partakers of the divine nature, and God is love (2 Peter 1:4; 1 John 4:16)! It is His most potent characteristic. It's His nature. That nature has been shed abroad in our hearts by the Holy Ghost (Rom. 5:5). And First Corinthians 13:7 in *The Amplified Bible* says, "Love bears up under anything and everything that comes . . . ."

Don't misunderstand me at all. I wouldn't preach something that I haven't practiced. From the natural standpoint, at times I've wanted to quit! I've been there! My mind was telling me, "You might as well quit." And more than once, naturally speaking, I *wanted* to quit.

But something on the inside wouldn't let me. Something on the inside of me—not only the Spirit of God, but the *love* of God—wouldn't allow it. To walk in the Spirit means to walk in love, and love bears up under anything and everything that comes!

Believing the Best

Paul continues on in First Corinthians, "Love . . . is ever ready to believe the best of every person . . ." (13:7 *Amplified*). Have you ever noticed that human nature is the opposite of that? Human nature seems to be always ready to believe the *worst* of every person. It seems to look for something to be wrong, and tries to make a case against someone.

But God's love is ever ready to believe the best. I like that, especially because if that's the way God's love is, then God is ever ready to believe the best about me! This God-kind of love is ever ready to believe the best of *every* person—husband, wife, brother, sister, children, friends, the pastor, or whomever.

For years, I traveled in what we used to call the field ministry. During World War II, I was out on the field in 1944 and '45. And from 1949 until 1974, when we started RHEMA Bible Training Center, I was constantly on the field. Traveling that much, I heard a lot of talk from ministers about other preachers. Some preacher would say, "Did you hear about Brother So-and-so?" And they would tell me something bad about him. I'd respond, "I refuse to believe the bad about anyone." And usually, I learned later that those comments weren't true. They were just rumors.

I refuse to believe the worst about anyone. Love is ever ready to believe the best of everyone. Children have a right, dear friend, to be brought up in a home with this kind of love atmosphere. When they are, they'll go out into the fight of life and win.

My wife and I maintained that kind of atmosphere in our home. That's why we never had any problems with our children. Oh, I don't mean that they didn't act like children. Of course they did. But we believed the best of them. When you see the worst in your children and always tell them about it, they'll never amount to anything. They'll live up to what you say. They may miss it, because you can't expect a child to behave like an adult. But when you see the best in them, and love them rightly, and bring the best out of them, they'll amount to something. And it's our responsibility as parents to do that, and to walk in love.

First Corinthians chapter 13 continues in *The Amplified Bible*, ". . . its [love's] hopes are fadeless under all circumstances, and it endures everything [without weakening]. Love never fails [never fades out or becomes obsolete or comes to an end]" (vv. 7,8).

We who are born again and baptized with the Holy Ghost are interested in spiritual gifts, and we should be. The Bible tells us to be interested in them (1 Cor. 12). But we should be interested in love first.

In First Corinthians chapter 13, Paul goes on to say that prophecies will fail, tongues will cease, and knowledge shall fall away. This doesn't mean that prophecies *have* failed. It just means that one day they will all have been fulfilled. It doesn't mean that tongues have ceased, but they will. There will be no need to talk in tongues in Heaven. And it doesn't mean that knowledge has fallen away. But one day, the need for more knowledge will. Thank God, though, *love never fails!*

Well, let's walk in love then. Once when I was at a restaurant with some ministers, they started talking about love. I just listened. (You learn more by listening.) I never said a word—never entered into the conversation. Now these were Full Gospel ministers and pastors. In fact, I was holding a meeting for one of them.

These ministers talked about how far short they, their congregations, and nearly everyone they knew was falling in walking in love. The pastor I was holding a meeting for said, "We need to pray that God would give us love. We just don't have the love we ought to have." I didn't say anything, but I thought, *Dear Lord, that's not true. They're just not walking in the light of what they have. That's where their problem is.*

Finally, this pastor that I was holding a meeting for asked me, "Brother Hagin, what do *you* think about it?"

"Do you really want to know?" I asked.

"Yes!" he said.

"Well, if you don't have any love, as you just got through saying, then you need to get saved."

That pastor looked at me as if I'd just slapped him with a wet dish rag.

I continued, "The Bible says, *'We know that we have passed from death unto life, because we love the brethren . . .'* [1 John 3:14]. And the Bible says, *'. . . the love of God is shed abroad in our hearts by the Holy Ghost . . .'*" (Rom. 5:5).

This man had been pastoring for several years. He looked up at me sort of startled and said, "Man! You are *right.*" Then he said, "I'll tell you what we need to do. We just need to pray that God would give us the baptism of love. We need to ask Him just to baptize us in love!"

I said, "Well, you're wrong again. There is no such thing as the baptism of love. Love is not a baptism; love is a *fruit.* Now I've been around you fellows, and I really don't see any fruit. But at least I see the bud. So don't get discouraged. I'm going to tell you how to bear fruit."

I began to tell them that if they'd keep feeding upon God's Word and fellowshipping with Him in prayer, they'd bear fruit. Jesus said, " *. . . He that abideth in me, and I in him, the same bringeth forth much fruit . . .*" (John 15:5). Well, love is a fruit. It's the first fruit of the Spirit listed in Galatians 5:22: *"But the fruit of the Spirit is* *love* . . . ." If a man says he doesn't have any love, then he is saying, in essence, "I'm not abiding in Him."

When these Full Gospel preachers got together, instead of talking about God and the things of God, they were more interested in talking about something else. Even in their spare time, instead of fellowshipping with the Lord, they'd play golf or do something else. I think it's all right to play golf if you want to. I have played a little bit, but not much. I don't have time.

And these pastors were constantly telling jokes. I think it's all right to tell something funny and enjoy one another's fellowship. But we need to put spiritual things first.

No, we don't need to pray for a baptism of love. We need to abide in Jesus, and let Him abide in us, through prayer and fellowship and communion with Him—waiting upon Him and feeding upon His Word. Then that love that is budding in our hearts will blossom and finally bring forth fruit.

So if all you can see in your life is just a few buds on the branch, don't get discouraged. Keep on abiding in Him and that fruit will mature.

Now God said if you will walk in His commandments and keep His statutes, He will take sickness away from the midst of you, and the number of your days He will fulfill. If you're dealing with any kind of sickness or disease, just do what the mother of that child who had seizures did. Just say, *Satan, you take your hands off my body. I'm walking in love. I'll fulfill the number of my days. Hallelujah!*

Make the following confession:

The love of God has been shed abroad in my heart by the Holy Ghost. I shall endeavor to let that love nature dominate me. I have God's love nature in my heart—in my spirit. I'll not let my natural, human reasoning dominate me. I refuse to allow the flesh to dominate me. I'm going to walk in the Spirit. I'm going to walk in love. I'm not a hater—I'm a lover. I'm walking in God's statute and commandment of love.

CHAPTER SIX

SUFFERING UNTO PERFECTION |

We've mentioned three things to be borne in mind regarding the Holy Ghost living *within* the believer. First, *constant renewals of the Spirit are necessary.* These are brought about by prayer, waiting on God, and feeding on His Word.

Second, it's important that we *walk in the Spirit,* so that He may keep us fully informed of the manner in which God would have us live.

Number Three:
The Way of The Spirit

Third, we should *learn the way of the Spirit* so that we can trace God in all of the circumstances that form our daily life with Him. In the next two chapters, we'll deal with this last point. We must learn the way of the Spirit.

Let's begin with the following verse in Isaiah chapter 55.

ISAIAH 55:9
9   For as the heavens are higher than the earth, so are my ways higher than your ways, and my thoughts than your thoughts.

God's thinking is not the same as ours. One great lesson to be learned by the born-again Christian is that God has His own way of working out His will in our lives.

Here is a side of truth we don't necessarily like to hear. (Discussing Bible truths is like climbing a mountain. You climb up one side and have one view, but if you climb up another side, you have another view.) Concerning Jesus, the Bible says that He was perfected by the things He suffered. Look at this passage in the Book of Hebrews.

HEBREWS 5:8–9
8   Though he were a Son, yet learned he obedience by the things which he suffered;
9   And being made perfect, he became the author of eternal salvation unto all them that obey him.

When we start talking about suffering, people get tangled up. They have done the same thing with suffering that they have done with the subject of prayer.

The Church as a whole has taken all prayer, put it in the same sack, shaken it up together, and poured it all out. But the Bible teaches that there are different kinds of prayer, and one kind can't take the place of another. Every kind is important in its place.

The same thing is true concerning suffering. People have put all kinds of suffering in a sack and shaken it up together, and they have become confused. But we need to see how the various kinds of suffering differ. Notice this passage in First Peter chapter 2.

> **1 PETER 2:18–19**
> **18 Servants, be subject to your masters with all fear; not only to the good and gentle, but also to the froward.**
> **19 FOR THIS IS THANKWORTHY, IF A MAN FOR CONSCIENCE** [conscience' sake] **TOWARD GOD ENDURE GRIEF, SUFFERING WRONGFULLY.**

When the Bible talks about suffering, it doesn't mean "sickness." We have no business suffering with or from sickness and disease, because Jesus redeemed us from that. Just a few verses after these, Peter wrote, ". . . *by whose stripes ye were healed*" (v. 24). Well, if we were healed, we are healed. But a lot of times, people who are sick say they are suffering for the Lord. No, they're not suffering for the Lord. But First Peter 2:19 does speak about enduring grief, suffering wrongfully.

> **1 PETER 2:20–21**
> **20 For what glory is it, if, when ye be buffeted for your faults, ye shall take it patiently? but if, when ye do well, and suffer for it, ye take it patiently, this is acceptable with God.**
> **21 For even hereunto were ye called: because Christ also suffered for us, LEAVING US AN EXAMPLE, THAT YE SHOULD FOLLOW HIS STEPS.**

We need to distinguish between the *example* of Christ in suffering, and the *substitution* of Christ in suffering. We can follow His *example* in suffering, but not His *substitution*, because as our Substitute, He took our place. As our Substitute, He suffered some things so that we wouldn't have to.

Notice the Bible says, *". . . leaving us an example, that ye should follow his steps"* (v. 21). How was Jesus our example in suffering?

1 PETER 2:22–23
22 Who did no sin, neither was guile found in his mouth:
23 Who, when he was reviled, reviled not again; WHEN HE SUFFERED, he threatened not; but committed himself to him that judgeth righteously.

In suffering death, in shedding His blood, in taking our sins upon Himself, Jesus was our Substitute. He suffered so we wouldn't have to. On the other hand, in His being reviled, persecuted, and spoken against, He suffered, and He served as our example in how to act when we are treated that way.

As Christians, we do suffer persecution. People talk about us; they revile us. That's what these verses are saying. When Jesus was reviled or spoken against by people, He didn't threaten them. He went right on. In the same way, when I'm criticized, I just keep putting out the truth; I don't take time to answer critics.

Think about what Jesus suffered. Philippians 2:7 says, *"But made himself of no reputation, and took upon him the form of a servant, and was made in the likeness of men."* That was a terrible price to pay, wasn't it? Think what He had to suffer to do that. Another translation says, "He laid aside His mighty power and glory and became as mere men." And another reads, "He laid aside all of His rights, His privileges, and His rightful dignity, and was born a human being."

Think about what that cost. He learned obedience through suffering. He was already obedient to the Cross. He didn't learn that; He was already obedient to come and do His Father's will. But He was made perfect through the things He suffered.

Hebrews 2:18 tells us Jesus suffered temptation: *"For in that he himself hath suffered being tempted, he is able to succour* [or aid] *them that are tempted."* We suffer temptation, don't we? But thank God, He is able to keep us. Jesus is able to succor those who are tempted because He was tempted in all points like we are.

We see that again in Hebrews chapter 4. Verse 15 says, *"For we have not an high priest which cannot be touched with the feeling of our infirmities; but was in all points tempted like as we are, yet without sin."* And the next verse says, *"Let us therefore come boldly unto the throne of grace, that we may obtain mercy, and find grace to help in time of need."*

Notice in Hebrews again, *"Who can have compassion on the ignorant, and on them that are out of the way; for that he himself also is compassed with infir-mity"* (Heb. 5:2). Jesus suffered temptation just as we do. Thank God, He can help us.

The Apostles Suffered

Let's look in the Book of Acts to see what is said there about suffering.

ACTS 5:41
41 And they departed from the presence of the council, rejoicing THAT THEY WERE COUNTED WORTHY TO SUFFER SHAME FOR HIS NAME.

This verse refers to the apostles who had been imprisoned and beaten for teaching in the Name of Jesus.

We don't suffer shame for the Name of Jesus in the United States like people sometimes do in other countries and like they did in the Early Church. But they rejoiced that they were counted worthy to suffer shame for His Name.

The ninth chapter of Acts tells of the conversion of Saul of Tarsus.

ACTS 9:10–16
10 And there was a certain disciple at Damascus, named Ananias; and to him said the Lord in a vision, Ananias. And he said, Behold, I am here, Lord.
11 And the Lord said unto him, Arise, and go into the street which is called Straight, and enquire in the

house of Judas for one called Saul, of Tarsus: for, behold, he prayeth,

12 And hath seen in a vision a man named Ananias coming in, and putting his hand on him, that he might receive his sight.

13 Then Ananias answered, Lord, I have heard by many of this man, how much evil he hath done to thy saints at Jerusalem:

14 And here he hath authority from the chief priests to bind all that call on thy name.

15 But the Lord said unto him, Go thy way: for he is a chosen vessel unto me, to bear my name before the Gentiles, and kings, and the children of Israel:

16 FOR I WILL SHEW HIM HOW GREAT THINGS HE MUST SUFFER FOR MY NAME'S SAKE.

Jesus said that. Now, Paul didn't suffer sickness and disease. That's where people get mixed up. What did he suffer? We find the answer in Second Corinthians.

2 CORINTHIANS 6:4–6

4   But in all things approving ourselves as the ministers of God, in much patience, in afflictions, in necessities, in distresses,

5   In stripes, in imprisonments, in tumults, in labours, in watchings, in fastings;

6   By pureness, by knowledge, by longsuffering, by kindness, by the Holy Ghost, by love unfeigned.

We talk about people being afflicted with sickness. But the Greek word translated "afflictions" in verse 4 means *tests or trials.*

In Second Corinthians chapter 11, we see more of what Paul suffered.

2 CORINTHIANS 11:23–28

23 Are they ministers of Christ? (I speak as a fool) I am more; in labours more abundant, in stripes above measure, in prisons more frequent, in deaths oft.
24 Of the Jews five times received I forty stripes save one.
25 Thrice was I beaten with rods, once was I stoned, thrice I suffered shipwreck, a night and a day I have been in the deep;
26 In journeyings often, in perils of waters, in perils of robbers, in perils by mine own countrymen, in perils by the heathen, in perils in the city, in perils in the wilderness, in perils in the sea, in perils among false brethren; [That's about the worst peril there is; it's difficult to suffer through too!]
27 In weariness and painfulness, in watchings often, in hunger and thirst, in fastings often, in cold and nakedness.
28 Beside those things that are without, that which cometh upon me daily, the care of all the churches.

That gives you some idea of the things Paul suffered. We don't suffer some of these things in the United States. But Paul did suffer them. Yet he was a man of faith; he had the right attitude. His faith carried him through all of those tests and trials.

Suffering Can Bring Maturity

Many people think that when they learn how to believe God, they'll never have any more problems. But the Bible doesn't teach that.

Suffering will make you grow up spiritually in a hurry. It's the same in the natural realm. As a child, your food and bed are provided—everything is furnished. But then it becomes time for you to get out on your own. You start paying rent, buying food, and making automobile payments. You find out right away whether you're mature or not.

As I look back now, I can see I wasn't aware that the Holy Spirit led me into many hard places. Just knowing the Word and walking by faith won't mature you. That's the reason many people never get settled or matured—they won't stay in a hard place. I thank God now for all those hard places He led me through. I thank God for the nosy people I've had to deal with.

One time we were having a "watch night" service in one church I pastored. At that type of service, people would stay until after midnight on December 31 to watch the New Year roll in. On this particular night, we didn't have any special speaker, and people were testifying about what different ones in the church meant to them.

I said, "I want to thank God for Sister So-and-so." Everyone looked at me, because Sister So-and-so was a gossip. She was a troublemaker and was always sticking her nose in everyone else's business. She caused everyone, including me, more problems and trouble than anyone else in the church did.

So I said, "I want to thank God for Sister So-and-so. She's been the greatest blessing to me of anyone in this church. She's kept me on my knees almost continually. I wouldn't have prayed nearly as much if it hadn't been for her."

Knowing her helped me! I suffered because of her, but it matured me.

Led by the Spirit Into the Wilderness

I want you to see how the Spirit of God sometimes is involved in these things. Jesus, you remember, was *led* by the Spirit into the wilderness to be tempted. Luke 4:1 says, *"And Jesus being full of the Holy Ghost returned from Jordan, AND WAS LED BY THE SPIRIT INTO THE WILDERNESS."*

(Here, by the way, is another type, or symbol, of the difference between being *born of* the Spirit and *baptized with* the Spirit. Jesus is our example. He was born of the Spirit. According to Luke 1:35, the Holy Spirit came upon Mary, and the power of God overshadowed her. Jesus was *born of* the Spirit. Then, thirty years later, we read in Luke chapter 4 that He was *baptized with* the Spirit, or anointed with the Holy Ghost, to do the works of God.)

So the Spirit led Jesus into the wilderness to be tempted of the devil. People want to accuse the devil of getting them into the wilderness. But Jesus was led there *by the Spirit.* That's what the Bible means when it says, "He was perfected through the things He suffered" (Heb. 5:8,9). Whether you realize it or not, these are the things that will make us or break us.

Here's where faith comes in. And here's also where the tragedy is. Sometimes, people listening to faith teachers get the idea that they will sail through life and everything will be "hunky-dory." They think they'll never have any trials, tests, or suffering of any kind. Then someone rises up and says something about them and they're ready to quit.

You're going to have persecution. Jesus said in John 16:33, *"These things I have spoken unto you, that in me ye might have peace. IN THE WORLD YE SHALL HAVE TRIBULATION: but be of good cheer; I have overcome the world."*

In the world you'll have tribulation, or persecution, or trouble. The devil will put up every roadblock he can. He could hinder more in the countries and provinces where Paul traveled because they didn't have the freedom of religion that we have.

People get this suffering business all mixed up. Someone gets double pneumonia and says, "I'm suffering for Jesus." That's not suffering for Jesus! Yet in some other areas, such as those listed in Mark chapter 10, suffering is coming our way.

MARK 10:28–30

28 Then Peter began to say unto him, Lo, we have left all, and have followed thee.

29 And Jesus answered and said, Verily I say unto you, There is no man that hath left house, or brethren, or sisters, or father, or mother, or wife, or children, or lands, for my sake, and the gospel's,

30 But he shall receive an hundredfold now in this time, houses, and brethren, and sisters, and mothers, and children, and lands, WITH PERSECUTIONS; and in the world to come eternal life.

We want to claim the houses and lands and blessings of God, but did you ever hear anyone say, "I'm claiming the *persecutions* in Mark chapter 10"? No, we always claim the *land*. And we do need to claim the land to get it. But you don't need to claim the persecutions—you'll get them anyway. Jesus said, "With prospering, you'll get persecuted."

You've read about people griping because a preacher had a nice house. What if he had a hundred homes? That would be scriptural. But I get enough persecution with just one—I wouldn't want another! People will criticize you, and if you haven't matured spiritually, that can throw you.

Suffering in the Ministry

I've been preaching for years that God wants *all* of His children—not just some of us, but *all* of us— healthy and healed. God wants us to live out our full length of time on earth without sickness and without disease. That's His best. Not everyone attains to it, but it's there for us anyway. You get criticized for preaching that.

For years I preached healing in Full Gospel churches, and sometimes the very pastor I would be preaching for would criticize me. Pastors would tell me, "Healing is not so important." One fellow in a meeting at which I was preaching said, "Healing was just a side issue with Jesus and the apostles." And he was a Full Gospel pastor! I kept preaching healing every night. I hammered down that same line. His remarks didn't bother me. I let them run off me like water off a duck's back.

These are things, dear friend, that build character. I've had storms come in from every side. The Spirit led me to preach a meeting for one fellow, even though I don't know why in the world he asked me to preach. He knew what I preached. I had heard him get up right in the middle of conventions and criticize what I was preaching. And here he was asking me to come hold a meeting. I said, "Lord, I don't want to go." There's some suffering that goes along with that kind of thing. Don't think it's all joy unspeakable and full of glory.

I remember starting off in that meeting by preaching something we could all believe in. I didn't try to be controversial. The pastor said, "You preach on texts I never heard anyone preach on." That's just me. I don't try to be someone else—I'm me. I had never in my life preached on the prodigal son, for instance. It's in the

Bible, and that's fine, but I've always preached on other texts. For this pastor, nearly everything I usually preached was controversial.

So I started out by going along with the people in order to get their attention. You have to be wise as a serpent and harmless as a dove (Matt. 10:16). I got their attention, and then I began to drop a little faith on them. I just gave them a spoonful occasionally—people can choke to death on too much. When I would see they were slipping from me, I'd get back on some old Baptist sermons like "The Marriage Supper of the Lamb" and "The Second Coming of Jesus." I'd get them with me again, and then I'd drop a little more faith on them.

I said, "Lord, why did You send me to this place to begin with?" I didn't know that you could hurt in so many places and still be in the will of God. But these are the things that will perfect you. They'll put some stamina in you. They'll give you a backbone like a crowbar instead of a cotton string. This is what it means to be led by the Spirit into the wilderness to be tempted of the devil—to be led by the Holy Spirit into a trial.

I remember something that happened when I was pastoring my last church. I was making plans to go to a fall Bible conference. I had preached on a Sunday night, and my wife and I were planning to leave for the conference the next Tuesday morning.

I stopped by my church office on Monday, and just as I started to go in, the Spirit of God said to me, "Fast the next two days. They're going to ask you to pray for the sick at the convention."

I stepped inside the church and said, "Well, Lord, if they do, that's going to be more than they ever did before. They haven't even asked me to pray about anything in the past. There are hundreds of preachers there." I was too "heavy" for some of them on some subjects.

My wife and I got to the conference on Tuesday and sat down in back because the building was full. In a little while, it was time for the main speaker to begin, and the fellow who was introducing him said, "I saw Brother Hagin come in awhile ago. The Lord has been dealing with me the last day or two to have him minister to the sick tonight—to have a healing meeting." He added that another man would be the main speaker for the evening, and asked me if I would prefer to have the healing service before or after the sermon. The Scriptures say to prefer your brother before yourself, so I said I would go afterward—and I made a mistake.

You talk about suffering! The speaker was upset because he thought I might ruin his sermon. He didn't like the idea of my having a healing service. He did choose a healing text—the woman with the issue of blood. And he did all right for awhile. He talked about miracles he'd seen in the early days of the Pentecostal movement.

But then he said, "I guess we shouldn't expect things like that in these times. Every movement is at its best in its beginning; then it starts to wane."

He began by getting people in faith, but wound up by getting them in the dark and in doubt, and then he turned the meeting over to me! There I was, having to wade through unbelief neck-deep. It was like swimming in something—and I didn't even swim in those days! I could hardly keep my head above water. The atmosphere was charged with unbelief. God wasn't expected to do what He ought to do. All the ministers on the platform were breathing that hot breath of unbelief down my neck. You talk about tough! Thank God, I don't have to put up with that anymore. I wouldn't go through that again for ten million dollars. But, on the other hand, I wouldn't take *twenty* million dollars for it.

That's the thing that gave me stamina—that perfected me. That was a kind of suffering. That's being led by the Spirit into the wilderness to be tempted of the devil.

CHAPTER SEVEN

A SUPERNATURAL CALL |

Some of the biggest trials I ever had were the result of pastoring the churches I pastored. And I was led by the Spirit to function as a pastor in them! Some of the biggest tests a minister faces come from fulfilling the call of God upon his life. The devil will throw up every kind of roadblock possible. If you don't have the stamina and character to suffer persecution and trials, you'll not make it. You'll fall by the wayside.

I remember one time I was holding a series of meetings for a minister friend of mine. He and his brother, also a minister, were originally from a certain church in east Texas. I had arranged to go there and hold a meeting the following week. That particular church was looking for a pastor and they had congregational rule; they would vote in the man they wanted. I had told the deacon board I would come by and preach for them.

I was holding night meetings at my minister friend's church, and every afternoon he and his brother would come by the church and we'd pray. They would always ask me if I had prayed about that church in east Texas. I would say, "No! I haven't even thought about it, much less prayed about it. I just take one day at a time." The Scriptures say, *"Take therefore no thought for the morrow,"* and, *"Sufficient unto the day is the evil thereof"* (Matt. 6:34).

I said, "It won't hurt me to go by there and preach. I don't know whether it's the will of God for me to take that church, and I'm not even interested in whether it's His will right now. I'm interested in this meeting we're having here." I don't get concerned about things like a lot of folks do.

On another afternoon we were praying in the church, and the pastor got a call to go to the hospital to visit someone. His brother went with him. I was walking up and down the aisles of the church, praying about the night meeting. I got to the back of the auditorium, stopped, and leaned on the end of a pew. Very casually I said, "Lord, I guess maybe I ought to start thinking about that church in east Texas. I'm not concerned about it—whatever You want is all right with me."

The voice of the Lord came unto me saying, "You're the next pastor of that church, and that's the last church you'll ever pastor." His voice was so plain, I almost turned around and said, "Who said that?"

I could have let the devil get hold of what the Lord had told me and thought, *I'm going to die! Or, I'll pastor there until I'm an old man—103—and then retire.* I didn't know what it meant and didn't take time to find out. I decided I would face what it meant when I got there.

About that time, the two preachers came in and asked me, "Have you prayed about east Texas?" I said, "You fellows are looking at the next pastor of that church."

They said, "You don't know that church like we do. It's split right down the middle. Half want the pastor to stay and half want him to leave. He can't stay unless he gets a two-thirds vote, and he only has half. The half that wants him to stay is mad at the half that wants him to go. Half of them sit on one side of the church and half on the other. They can't get together on anything. You don't know that church like we do."

I said, "No, I don't know that church, but I do know Jesus and the Holy Spirit. And the Lord told me, 'You're the next pastor there.'"

That next week, I took the whole family with me to that town and we went to the home of one of the deacons. He said, "Brother and Sister Hagin, we'd be glad to have you stay with us the whole time you're here, but if you did, some would think I was for you. They'd vote against you. You'd better go somewhere else tomorrow night." So, we stayed with another one of the board members the next night. And he said, "Brother Hagin, I'm glad you can stay with us, but some may think we're for you if you stay more than one night. They might vote against you. You had better go somewhere else."

We stayed different places, and one night I whispered to my wife, "Do you know what I'd do if I didn't know God was in this? I'd get up in the middle of the night, and we'd leave and wouldn't tell anyone we're going." But knowing that God had led me there held me steady. I was perfected through what I suffered.

I'm reminded of a verse of Scripture in First Peter chapter 5.

> **1 PETER 5:10**
> **10 But the God of all grace, who hath called us unto his eternal glory by Christ Jesus, AFTER THAT YE HAVE SUFFERED A WHILE, make you perfect, stablish, strengthen, settle you.**

We need to learn the way of the Spirit, dear friend. And He doesn't always lead in a bed of roses or where the going is good. He doesn't always lead where there's smooth sailing and no opposition or persecution. But if you'll hold steady, you'll come out on top.

Another Opportunity to Prove God

Do you know why I'm so settled? It's because I suffered awhile. You'll even begin to praise God for trials and tests when you learn about them. Each one is just another opportunity to prove God.

When I was preaching at that church in east Texas, we stayed with a different member each night. A time or two, we even slept on the floor.

I started preaching there on a Wednesday night. You talk about suffering through a service! Thank God for my Baptist training. As a Baptist I had learned to preach from an outline, and I kept that outline right in front of me. It was a good thing, too, or I would have forgotten everything I knew.

I went through that outline—one, two, three—and every word I spoke came back and slapped me in the face. By the time I got to the last point, I felt like someone had been beating me in the face. After some of these meetings, my wife said, "I feel like someone has been beating me all over with his fists."

You just have to suffer through some of these things. Remember that Christ was made perfect through the things He suffered. The Greek word translated "perfect" also means *mature.* Christ was made perfect or reached maturity. Whether you like it or not, these are the things that mature us. We need to learn the way of the Spirit. He'll lead you into things like that. Jesus, full of the Holy Ghost, was led by the Spirit into the wilderness to be tempted or tested of the devil.

I originally thought I would only have to preach at that church in east Texas that one Wednesday night. But the church board told me they wanted me to preach every night through Sunday. They said, "After Sunday night, we'll have an election."

I knew the Lord had said, "You're going to pastor that church." But I thought, *I wish He hadn't said that! I'd leave!* I was so glad I had learned to preach from notes. I would feel anointed, but the minute I stepped inside the church door, it was as if someone had poured a bucket of cold water on me. Finally, I said to my wife, "I'll go out there and throw out a little dry hay for the people, and we'll go home." That was about all I could do.

We went on through Sunday night, and the deacon board said, "What do you think about it?" I said, "Well, go ahead and vote." I never did tell them God sent me. I didn't want them to know that the Lord led me into such a mess. I said, "The church has got to have its way about it."

They had their election, and I got every vote but two. People said, "It's a miracle that church could ever get together on anyone."

So I started pastoring that church. You talk about a fellow suffering! I suffered for the first six months. I never said anything in front of our two children. They thought everything was wonderful. But practically every Sunday night when I got in bed, I'd whisper to my wife, "If I didn't know God was in this, you know what I'd do? I'd rent a truck, back it up to the parsonage in the middle of the night, load up our things, and leave. I wouldn't tell a soul. People would come by the parsonage the next day and find it empty. They'd say, 'I wonder where Hagin went?' They'd know the Rapture hadn't taken place because the furniture would be gone too."

In the natural, that's what I would have done. But I stayed and suffered.

But because the Lord led me to this church, I learned many valuable lessons which have stood me in good stead over the years. Those lessons really helped me as I preached the message of faith when it wasn't popular. It's not too popular in some areas even today. Yet I stayed with it.

I preached that God wants us to prosper. At that time, I had only one pair of shoes, and they had holes in them. I had a dime in one pocket and a hole in the other. The automobile I was driving had four bald tires and no spare. Finally, the car wore out and I sold it for junk and lit out on foot. But I stayed with it.

One would not choose such a way to grow in grace. But God sees differently than we do.

What happens to many people when trials and tests come? They say, "I don't know why this is happening to me. I'm trying my best, God knows." But when they know the Word of God, they'll look the trials and tests in the face and say, "Glory to God! Hallelujah! Here's another opportunity to live by faith—to prove God. Here's another opportunity to prove the Bible is true!"

Great Faith Comes Out of Great Tests

Smith Wigglesworth said, "Great faith comes out of great tests." We read, "*. . . faith cometh by hearing, and hearing by the word of God*" (Rom. 10:17). Of course, you can believe what God's Word has promised you. But great faith doesn't come just by feeding on God's Word. Great faith doesn't come just by hearing cassette tapes. The *potential* for great faith comes by hearing. But great faith itself comes when you put what you have heard into practice.

You see, faith is a force. To build up faith muscles, you have to use your faith against something. You don't build up muscles in your body just by reading books on building muscles, do you? No! It's when you put into practice what you read and start lifting weights that the muscles begin bulging out. Some folks have read all my books on faith, but they don't have a faith muscle yet. They've listened to every tape. But if all their faith were dynamite, it wouldn't be enough to blow their noses! *You've got to put the force of faith against a test!*

That's why after you grow a little bit, you begin to thank God for the tests. Great faith comes out of great tests. Wigglesworth also said, "Great victories come out of great battles." I know Jesus won the victory for us over the devil. He did it for us vicariously. But you've still got battles to fight, dear friend. No army ever won a great victory without having a battle. No boxer ever became heavyweight champion of the world without fighting someone—without having a great battle.

When you learn that great victories come out of great battles, you can praise the Lord in the middle of the test. You already know the outcome—you know you are going to overcome. Overcoming faith belongs to us. It is ours.

We need to learn the way of the Spirit, because sometimes He'll lead us in ways our natural mind doesn't like. In pastoring for twelve years, I never did pastor a church I really wanted to pastor.

Another Troubled Church

I received the baptism of the Holy Spirit as a Baptist preacher. But then I received the "left foot of fellowship" from among the Baptists and came over among the Pentecostals. I held a meeting one time in a certain Pentecostal church, and the Lord began to deal with me about pastoring it. It was in nearly as big a mess as the church I was already pastoring. And I was led by the Spirit into that one too.

The minister of that church wrote me a letter and said, "Brother Hagin, I'm leaving this church. The board asked me to write you and ask if you would consider pastoring it. You preached here a whole month once, so if you'll just consider taking it, they'll put your name up for a vote."

I wrote back and said, "Yes." I didn't say God had dealt with me already, but I said I would consider taking it.

So they voted me in unanimously and I went there to pastor. And you wouldn't believe the mess I got into! You wouldn't believe all I suffered through. It hurt! But the Lord led me into the wilderness to be tempted of the devil.

At that time, I was just twenty-one years old. The church had been there twenty-three years and some members had been baptized in the Holy Spirit for that length of time—longer than I was old! In all those years, they had never supported a pastor; he'd always had to work for a living. I was the first pastor they ever supported. I learned later that this had been a troubled church. No one would have it. The Spirit of God had led me to take it, though.

I'll be honest with you—pastoring that first church in Pentecostal circles had more to do with the success of my ministry today than anything else. I was perfected through the things I suffered.

When I would try to get an evangelist to come hold a meeting at that church, no one would do it. I couldn't get anyone. Finally, a friend of mine said, "Bless your heart, Brother Hagin, you don't know it, but I preached a three-week revival there, and they gave me only a dime." A dime! Ten cents! That had spread among all the evangelists and they had said, "Don't go there. You'll lose your shirt and tie and everything else!"

Finally, I had to say to some of them, "I'll guarantee you such-and-such amount." I didn't tell them I would take it out of my own pocket if necessary.

I got some of them to come. (You couldn't blame them for hesitating.) We grew as a church, and God blessed us. When I left, more than forty preachers put their names in for that church. They wanted it *then*. But they didn't want that mess before.

Don't Magnify the Suffering

I was preaching a meeting in a Full Gospel church one time, and the pastor invited me to stay for a missionary rally after my meetings were finished.

The missionary told how he had gone to a certain country. In seven years he had only helped two people receive Jesus as Lord. He came home discouraged, but God told him to go back. He went again, and in one year's time got 240,000 saved, and 70,000 baptized with the Holy Spirit. And he started 50 churches. That's pretty good, isn't it?

All of this missionary's report was good. Afterward, he showed pictures of some of his revivals. Finally, he opened the meeting up for questions. One minister's wife said, "Brother, I notice you always tell something good. Other missionaries talk about persecution. Don't you ever get persecuted? Others talk about getting thrown in jail. Does that ever happen to you?"

I remember he looked up at me and grinned. He said, "I do like Brother Hagin does. Of course, we suffer those things, but we don't magnify them. We tell about the good side."

I think that's what we do with the faith message. We tell about the good. But people don't realize some of these other things exist.

The missionary said, "I've had rotten eggs thrown right in my face while I was preaching. I've had rotten tomatoes thrown in my face. I've been arrested. We've been threatened with jail."

He added, "There is a native worker who is field superintendent over the missions work in the country where I minister. Because he and I are Christians, we don't bet. But we have a little joke going. We have our suitcases packed, and we jokingly say to one another, 'I'm going to get thrown in jail for preaching the Gospel before you do.'"

Paul was put in jail. And if he had griped and complained, he would have stayed in jail. Yet because he was full of faith, he and Silas began to sing praises to God at midnight, and they got out! (See Acts16:25–26).

We need to preach both sides. Tests and trials do come, but we must remember there is victory in Jesus! And it is also good to remember that some of our hardest tests are God's way of leading us into a deeper place in Him.

That first church I pastored was a problem! I learned later that *every* church I pastored was a troubled church. I asked the Lord one day, "Why do You always lead me to those places?" He didn't say so, but I think He knew I could take it. And He knew I needed the experience.

My ministry wouldn't be what it is today if I hadn't pastored that first church. And it wouldn't be what it is if I hadn't pastored my last church. Some of the hardest tests I've gone through in more than sixty-five years of experience were because I was led by the Spirit of God. He knew the test was coming. It was God's way of teaching me.

Thank God for the written Word, but you can't learn some things just by reading the written Word. It's when you put the Word into practice that it becomes real to you.

You can sit around all day and holler, "My God shall supply all my needs," and starve to death while you are hollering it if you're just hollering and not believing in your heart, and not doing your part in the natural. Paul wrote that to the believers in Philippi. They were *givers*. They'd already acted on what they heard Paul preach by giving to him. (See Phil. 4:15–19.)

I've seen people holler all day long, "He took my infirmities and bare my sicknesses," but they aren't really believing anything. They are just mentally assenting to God's Word, which says, ". . . *Himself took our infirmities, and bare our sicknesses*" (Matt. 8:17). Thank God He did. But when you put the Word into practice and enjoy the results of it, then you know what you are talking about.

Suffering Because of God's Call

Some folks have it mighty easy in this day and time. But I feel sorry for folks who have always had it easy.

You know, it was hard for me to go out into field ministry. At the church we were pastoring at the time, our home had been like Heaven on earth for ten years. Now I was going to have to be gone ninety percent of the time. That's something to suffer through!

After I left that church and went into field ministry, my wife raised the children. She is to be commended. I get the credit for it, but she did it. She's the one who instilled the right principles in them.

When I went out in the field, Ken was in the third grade and Pat was in the second grade. I wasn't with them all those years through grade school. Then when they became teenagers, I wasn't with them much of the time. I had always looked forward with great anticipation to

family life. The day after Ken was born, I asked
Oretha, "When will he be old enough for me to carry
him with me?"

It's tough to be out on the road by yourself, shut up
in a hotel room, staring at the four walls. But God said,
"Do it!"

When Ken got to be about twelve years old, I
would take him with me sometimes. I remember once
we were driving back to Texas after a service in Oklahoma. We got home, and that night as we were kneeling by the bed to pray, Ken began to cry and he asked
me, "Daddy, why do you have to be gone all the time?
Why can't you be home like other daddies?" That's
tough to take!

I tried not to be gone. I stayed out on the field for
seven months and, finally, I said, "It's too rough. It's
too big a price to pay. I won't pay it. I'll go back to
pastoring. I'll be with my family."

I cancelled my meetings. Cancelled my meetings!
On Sunday, July 10, 1949, I was planning to preach at
a church in east Texas. It was one of the best churches
in the area. I had been assured I could have it if I
wanted it.

My wife and I went there that day, and I attended a
men's Bible class before the service. I was sitting on a
bench and, suddenly, my heart stopped and I pitched
over onto the floor on my face. I fell right at the pastor's feet.

He picked me up and my heart began to race. You couldn't detect the beating. It felt like something shaking—like a bowl full of gelatin.

Some people carried me over to the parsonage next door. I said, "Feel my heart." They felt it and began to cry. Two more preachers came over. They told me later, "We just knew you were dead." I was cold all over and white as a sheet. Death was upon my brow.

The ministers ran to the Sunday school addition and one of them motioned to my wife. She was already getting up. She told them, "The Lord spoke to me and told me something had happened to him."

She rushed in and fell on her knees beside the bed.

She said, "I feel like this is my fault! I was complaining to God because you were gone all the time. And I heard a voice speak while I was washing the dishes. It said, 'I could take him where he would never come back.' I looked all through the house—under the bed and behind the door in the bathroom. I couldn't find anyone. I checked the doors and they were locked. I just decided I was hearing things."

Kneeling there by the bed I lay on, she prayed, "Lord, that was You who spoke to me in an audible voice. I'll never complain anymore. I don't care how long he's gone or where he goes." Then I made my consecration: "I'll do what You said to do, Lord."

The power of God fell on us. The power of God fell on *me* and I was instantly healed! I leaped off that bed and danced through the house.

Now, you remember I had cancelled all my meetings. I didn't have a meeting left, yet I had a wife and two children to support, and rent and utilities to pay.

You may ask, "Why didn't you just take a job?" I did do that at first. But I never lost sight of my calling. I was in the ministry and was living by faith. So I'd take any meeting, wherever the door opened. We had some of the most miraculous things happen.

I feel sorry for folks who have never had such a privilege. Some people are driving Cadillacs and living big, and they think they are living by faith. They are no more living by faith than I'm an astronaut. They talk about the faith life while drinking malted milks and eating T-bone steaks!

Now, they may get there after awhile. Don't misunderstand me. But we had the biggest time just obeying God. I think that was one of the sweetest times of our lives. And it was a time of great spiritual growth.

We lived from week to week and hardly knew where our next meal was coming from. But we were never in lack, because our confidence and faith were in the Lord.

Learn the way of the Spirit, friend. When I went out on the road, I fought more devils in that first seven months than I had in the previous fifteen years of ministry put together! If the devil could have kept me out of that field ministry, he could have kept me out of where we are now. I'd have given up on it. But I learned through what I suffered.

We don't like to hear that side of it too much. But when the Lord has told you something, stay hooked up with what He's said to you. Go right on through the tests and trials and be perfected.

Although we may not suffer physical persecution in the United States the way Paul suffered, some of our brethren in other countries may have to undergo some of those same things he did.

You may be called to a foreign field. You may have to suffer some things too. You may not have all the modern conveniences. You may be in an area where there is no electricity or running water. Don't tell me that's easy, because I know it's not. But if God calls you, there will be joy in it. The Lord will bless you.

When I went out on the field, I told Ken, "Here's why I have to be gone. Your mother and I have made a dedication to the Lord. God said to go. He'll make it up to us." Jesus said in Mark chapter 10 that He would.

MARK 10:29–30
29 And Jesus answered and said, Verily I say unto you, There is no man that hath left house, or brethren, or sisters, or father, or mother, or wife, or children, or lands, for my sake, and the gospel's,
30 But he shall receive an hundredfold now in this time, houses, and brethren, and sisters, and mothers, and children, and lands, with persecutions; and in the world to come eternal life.

God certainly did make it up to us in so many ways. I was preaching years later at a Full Gospel church in Cushing, Oklahoma. In the night, I suddenly sat bolt upright in bed. I knew immediately that Ken's life was in danger. He was in the Army at that time, serving in Taiwan. That night he had been riding a motorcycle, and the front wheel had gone off a mountain. It was a thousand feet to the bottom. If he had gone over the cliff, he would have been killed.

When I sat up in bed, the Lord said to me, "You obeyed Me. If you hadn't, he would never come back from Taiwan. But you obeyed Me. He'll be back."

So God made it up to me. Yet I suffered during those years of field ministry. Many times when I left, I would be weeping by the time I drove the car around the corner. I would weep all the way to my next meeting. I'd rather have been at home. There's a price to pay, dear friend, to obey God. But, glory to God, we'll not magnify the suffering. I like to be around when payday comes! It wasn't easy back then. Some people want to start out where I am today. In some ways you can, and in some ways you can't. But after you have suffered a little while and have been faithful, it will pay off.

I don't often share these things. I've said, "I'm a faith person—my faith saw me through." But the Lord talked to me about telling this part too. We've got to tell the other side.

It takes faith to go through these trials. Many times, after meetings at night, I would get so lonely. You are by yourself so much. I've actually thought about getting up and kicking out the windowpanes for a little excitement!

If you think that's not suffering, go through it and you'll find out. Yes, there is suffering, but not with sickness and disease. Thank God, you don't have to suffer with that, because Jesus bore our infirmities. He suffered that for us as our Substitute, not as our example.

It costs something to be faithful to God. It costs something to separate yourself unto the ministry God has called you to. But the foundation for my ministry today came in my staying put in the hard places where God led me. I stayed in places where I didn't want to stay. That's where I learned so much. That's when the foundation was established in me.

Learn the way of the Spirit. Let God have His way in your life. Stay put in the hard places, and you will eventually rest upon the mountaintop.

CHAPTER EIGHT

*H*OLY SPIRIT ADVENTURES

As we have seen, there is a twofold working of the
Spirit of God in the life of the believer. The Holy Spirit
comes *within* the believer in the New Birth; and the
Spirit comes *upon* the believer in the baptism with the
Holy Spirit.

The Holy Spirit *within* has to do with the personal
state of the believer more than with service or witnessing or power. The personal state of the believer accomplished by the work of the Spirit *within* can be referred
to as *holiness*. And the work of the Spirit *upon* the
believer, coming in the baptism with the Holy Spirit,
has to do with service or witnessing. It is a baptism of
power.

Of course, we would not for one moment despise
the power which comes with the baptism in the Holy
Ghost. But often there is too little said about holiness.
We're in danger of being overbalanced by an emphasis
on power, leaving God's people in the dark as to His
expectation for their personal walk with Him.

As we pointed out earlier in this book, the Holy
Spirit working *within* the believer produces fruit. And
the very first fruits are love, joy, peace, and the other
characteristics found in Galatians chapter 5, verses 22
and 23.

So when Christ told his disciples that the Holy Spirit *". . . dwelleth with you, and shall be IN you"* (John 14:17), He had a real experience in mind. And when Jesus told His disciples, *". . . tarry ye in the city of Jerusalem, until ye be endued with power from on high,"* (Luke 24:49), He had another real experience in mind.

We've looked at some length at the subject of the Holy Spirit within the believer. Now let's consider the subject of the Holy Spirit upon the believer.

We've seen that being born again and having the Holy Spirit come within the believer is a definite experience which we should enjoy. In the same way, there is also a genuine outpouring of the Holy Spirit which God gives to those who will accept it and believe Him for it. God will do this for believers today just as He did for the 120 disciples gathered together on the Day of Pentecost. This experience is still available.

In John 20:22, Jesus breathed on the disciples and said, *". . . Receive ye the Holy Ghost."* And Luke 24:45 says, *"Then opened he their understanding, that they might understand the scriptures."* Notice that this happened *after* the resurrection of the Lord Jesus Christ, but *before* the outpouring of the Holy Ghost on the Day of Pentecost.

When Jesus breathed on the disciples and said, "Receive ye the Holy Ghost," it is quite evident that something transpired within them. Up to this time, they were a mystified and troubled group. But after meeting with the risen Christ, their condition changed. And even before the Holy Ghost was poured out upon them on the Day of Pentecost, Luke says, *". . . they wor-shipped him, and returned to Jerusalem with great joy: And were continually in the temple, praising and blessing God"* (Luke 24:52–53).

Remember, one of the fruits of the Presence of the Holy Spirit within is joy. This change came about by the Spirit of Christ who was now dwelling within them.

An Enduement of Power

In addition to this blessing, however, the Lord commanded his disciples to tarry in Jerusalem until they were endued with power from on high. Notice that Jesus did not tell them to tarry in Jerusalem until they were converted, or born again, or made new creatures, or regenerated (these are different terms for the same experience). He didn't even tell them to tarry until they received the Holy Spirit. He had already breathed on them and said, *". . . Receive ye the Holy Ghost"* (John 20:22). But He *did* say, *". . . tarry ye in the city of Jerusalem until ye be endued with POWER . . ."* (Luke 24:49). In Acts 1:8 Jesus said, *"But ye shall receive POWER, after that the Holy Ghost is come upon you . . . ."*

Paul wrote his Epistles to churches that had received not only the New Birth, but also this enduement of power. As Christians, we realize we're born again; the Spirit bears witness with our spirits that we are children of God (Rom. 8:16). But often as we read the Epistles, it seems like we don't have what the Early Church had. We seem to be so powerless.

I remember preaching a number of years ago at a Full Gospel Business Men's Fellowship meeting in a certain city. I spoke just one night, but for five nights, each service dealt with the baptism in the Holy Ghost.

During the meeting, a Baptist pastor came forward and was baptized in the Holy Ghost. Later as we talked he said, "Now I can go back to pastoring." He explained that he used to pastor a Baptist church in another city in that state, and from every standpoint, it appeared that he should have been satisfied. He had a large church and was well taken care of financially. He was well-educated—he had college degrees and had graduated from a Baptist seminary.

But this man said, "I pastored for about twelve years, and the longer I pastored, the more powerless I felt. I was taught in seminary that I was born of the Spirit and already had the Holy Ghost, and that was all there was to it. But the more I read the Book of Acts and the Epistles, the more I thought, *If I have what they had, it sure doesn't work with me like it did with them.*" He was sensible and reasonable enough to see that the Scriptures referred to something other than what he was experiencing.

That pastor continued, "People came to me for help, and I felt so powerless. I just didn't have it. I knew I was saved, but finally I decided I couldn't go on."

He and his wife had two children in their early teens. After struggling with the issue for about a month, he called his family together and told them what he had on his mind. He told them he wasn't quitting God, because God was real to him. But he told them he felt so tired in the ministry, and that with his education, he could go into business. In fact, he'd already been offered certain positions.

So this man took a business position and did well financially. But he got interested in the baptism with the Holy Ghost through the Full Gospel Business Men's Fellowship. He said, "I didn't understand it. I'd spoken against the Pentecostal movement. But I finally got so hungry spiritually that I told the Lord, 'Okay. If it takes tongues, I'm ready for that too.'" He came forward during the meeting I was preaching and was gloriously baptized in the Holy Ghost and spoke with other tongues. And he said to me, "Praise God, I just can't wait to get back into the ministry!" You see, he was ready for it then.

Jesus' disciples, including the apostles, were called and ordained of God. But He told them, "Don't you leave Jerusalem until you are endowed with *power* from on high."

I was born and raised as a Southern Baptist. I remember hearing years ago of a professor at Baylor University seminary. He was an old, white-haired gentleman. He would say to each seminary graduating class, "There is an experience subsequent to salvation called the baptism of the Holy Ghost. It is an endue-ment of power from on high. And don't you dare go out and preach without it." That was about all he dared say about it. But if he could arouse their curios-ity and get them seeking God, great things could happen. He was just following Jesus' admonition to His disciples.

The One and Only Way

Now I want to reiterate a few thoughts. It's rather significant that we have two groups of nine connected with the work of the Holy Spirit. We looked at these briefly earlier, and went into some depth about love. In Galatians 5:22 and 23, we see nine fruit of the Spirit. They might be referred to as character traits resulting from the *indwelling* Presence of the Holy Spirit. Jesus said, *"I am the vine, ye are the branches . . ."* (John 15:5). Fruit grows on the branch because of the life within the tree, doesn't it? So as a result of the indwelling of the Spirit, we have the ninefold fruit of the Spirit.

Then in First Corinthians 12:7–11, we are taught that the manifestation of the Spirit is given to every man, and here also we have a group of nine. We often call these the nine manifestations or *gifts* of the Spirit. These are given *" . . . to profit withal . . ."* (1 Cor. 12:7). In other words, the gifts of the Spirit are given so that believers can bless others.

From this, one easily can draw the conclusion that the *indwelling* of the Spirit, coming in the New Birth, is for *fruit-bearing*, and the *outpouring* of the Spirit, coming in the baptism with the Holy Spirit, is for *service*.

This introduces us to the thought that the baptism with the Holy Spirit, as taught in Acts 2:1–4, is *the one and only way* in which we are given the complete ninefold manifestation of the Spirit.

The Spirit Within Still Leads

Now, it's true that after I was born again but before I was baptized in the Holy Spirit, the Spirit in me would lead me. Romans 8:14 says, *"For as many as are led by the Spirit of God, they are the sons of God."* The Holy Spirit *in* me would tell me things and show me things and direct me. I'd know about certain things and be able to pray about them ahead of time. But there's a vast difference between that and being baptized in the Holy Ghost and having supernatural manifestations like the word of knowledge operating through me.

Now, many people make a mistake here. When our spirit is born again and in fellowship with God, the Holy Spirit dwells in us, and our spirit will automatically sense some things. A lot of people don't understand that. Many of them have been born again and plunged almost immediately into the baptism in the Holy Ghost. They think the word of knowledge is operating through them because their spirits pick up certain things. But we know certain things in our born-again spirit that are not necessarily coming through the supernatural manifestation or gift of the word of knowledge.

I'll give you an illustration. I was born again on April 22, 1933, but I remained bedfast for another sixteen months before I was healed. In early August of 1933, I was about sixteen years old. My oldest brother, Dub, who would be eighteen that September, had left home.

These were the days of the Great Depression and work was hard to find. Dub told some family members that he planned to go down to the Rio Grande River Valley and see if he could find work. In those days, boys would hop a freight train to travel and look for jobs. Those trains were full of young men. People called them hoboes.

Well, while Dub was gone, I sensed in my spirit that his life was in danger. I didn't mention it to my mother. I thought she had enough problems with my being bedfast. She had to wait on me like she would a baby.

Finally, after three days, Momma said to me, "Son, I hate to bother you in your physical condition, but I'm greatly troubled about Dub. He's in trouble some way or another, and I don't know what it is." You see, her spirit also picked up that Dub was in trouble. She told me she thought he might have been arrested and put in jail.

I said, "No, Momma, that's not it. You're not telling me anything I don't already know. I've known for three days and didn't want to bother you about it. He's not in jail. His physical life was in jeopardy. But I've been praying for three days about it, and I have peace about it. He's all right. Forget it."

I knew that by a sort of inward intuition—an inward witness. Remember, Romans 8:14 says, *"For as many as are led by the Spirit of God, they are the sons of God."* And verse 16 of that same chapter says, *"The Spirit itself* [or Himself] *beareth witness with our spirit, that we are the children of God."* That witness comes in the New Birth. Well, the same Spirit that bears witness with your spirit that you're a child of God will bear witness with your spirit about other things.

So I just had that inward intuition, that inward witness, that my brother's physical life was in danger. But I'd prayed about it and knew he was all right. I told Momma, "I have peace in my spirit about it. I've got the answer."

Momma asked, "Are you sure, son? Are you sure?" We were babies in these things.

I said, "I've never been any more sure of anything in my life. Just be at rest. He's fine."

She sighed with relief and said, "Oh, I'm glad to hear that!"

A little more than twenty-four hours after that conversation, Dub came home at night. He had been riding a freight train back from the Rio Grande Valley. He was between Corsicana, Texas, and Dallas when a railroad detective knocked him in the head with a blackjack and threw him off the train.

In 1933, railroad locomotives still burned coal, and there were cinders along the track. The last thing Dub remembered was scooting along on his back on those rough cinders. They tore his shirt completely off and ripped out the seat of his pants. The fall nearly broke his back, and his bottom and back were burned raw.

Some hours later, Dub regained consciousness. He was lying in a ditch, and was sore all over. The fall would have killed him if Momma and I hadn't known about it in the Spirit and prayed.

Now Dub had no shirt or undershirt. The upper part of his body was naked. The whole seat of his pants and his underwear were gone, and his bottom was sticking out. In those days, you couldn't go out like that in public. They would arrest you for indecent exposure. He couldn't thumb a ride on the highway, and he couldn't go out in the daytime. So for three days, he walked up the railroad tracks, traveling at night. In the daytime, he'd hide in someone's field or orchard. At that time of year, some watermelons and other fruit were ripe, so he'd eat whatever he could get. He walked through Dallas at night so he wouldn't be arrested, then walked home along the railroad track.

As I said, Dub had rolled around in those cinders, and his back and bottom had been scraped raw—red and black. He looked black all over. He was dirty. He was so sore, he couldn't get out of bed for two or three days. But, you see, Momma and I knew by an inward intuition—and thank God for it—that something had happened to him.

Someone might say, "You knew that because you are a prophet." That has nothing to do with the prophet's ministry. I didn't enter into the ministry of the prophet until the 1950s. I knew simply through the Spirit of God in my born-again spirit that something had happened to Dub. Not one member of my family has ever been in trouble or near death without my knowing about it ahead of time. Sometimes in the night, the Spirit of God would awaken me and alert me.

$\mathcal{A}$ Deeper Dimension |

Being baptized in the Holy Spirit brings you into a deeper dimension of the Spirit. For the sake of illustration, you could explain it like this. Being born again, of course, is necessary. But having the Spirit of God in the New Birth is like an adult going swimming in a child's swimming pool.

The water in a child's swimming pool is about twelve to eighteen inches deep. But being baptized in the Holy Spirit is like going over into the adult swimming pool where the water goes all the way from three or four feet deep to eight to ten feet deep or deeper. It's the same Spirit, but in a deeper dimension. And in this dimension, among other things, the Holy Ghost can help you to pray, and you can get the answer much more easily.

I want you to understand that, according to the Scriptures, it is possible to come behind in no gift. Paul said to the Church at Corinth, "*. . . ye come behind in no gift . . .*" (1 Cor. 1:7).

A deep Pentecostal experience such as the baptism in the Holy Spirit is not to be despised, but rather coveted. And it is the *one way* to enter into the fullness of God.

At the time I was baptized in the Holy Spirit, I was pastor of a church. People were saved in that church and because I had been healed, I taught that you could be healed in answer to faith. In line with Mark 11:24, I taught that if you'd pray and believe when you pray, you'd receive. I laid hands on people and even anointed them with oil, and we saw people healed.

But in that church, we never had one single manifestation of the gifts of the Spirit among us. We never had any prophecy. I'd get anointed to preach, of course, because with the calling of God, the anointing is there. But we never had any tongues and interpretation, or discerning of spirits, or words of knowledge. But as soon as I was baptized with the Holy Ghost, we began to see supernatural manifestations. And, eventually, nearly every member of the congregation followed me in receiving the baptism in the Holy Spirit.

Two things are involved here. Jesus said, *". . . ye shall receive power, after that the Holy Ghost is come upon you . . ."* (Acts 1:8). In those days, Pentecostal people particularly emphasized power. Because I knew the Scriptures, I knew that I had received the baptism in the Holy Spirit because I spoke with tongues. I knew that tongues were supernatural. But after I received that experience, sometimes when I was alone, I'd pinch myself and think, *If I've got any more power, I can't tell it.* I didn't feel any more powerful than I did before.

We Each Must Be Led by the Spirit

Everyone has to be led by the Spirit for himself. You can't tell someone else what to do. We make a mistake when we do that. I don't have much respect for people who are always "getting leadings" for the other fellow.

Sometimes I know things by the Spirit and I drop a few hints. But I won't just tell a fellow something unless God tells me to tell him. He needs to learn for himself how God leads. He doesn't need to lean on someone else, because that will hold him in bondage and keep him, or her, a baby Christian. And Christians need to grow and develop.

I was led by the Spirit not to say anything to my church about being baptized in the Holy Spirit. I didn't just blurt out, "I've got the baptism in the Holy Ghost now. I speak with tongues!"

Some Baptist minister friends of mine received this experience and just had to tell it. They went right back to their churches all exuberant, and the next Sunday morning, they began to talk about it. And after they preached their sermons, their church boards threw them out, and they never got to tell anyone else about it. That was the end of it.

On the other hand, a Methodist pastor friend of mine received this experience and went a different way with it. He was baptized in the Holy Spirit while visiting an Episcopalian meeting. While returning home, he began to think about it. He thought, *Dear Lord, what am I going to do? If I tell this to my church, I'll be thrown out. I don't even dare tell my wife about it.*

So he prayed, and he told me that it seemed like the Lord said to him, "Just keep quiet about it for awhile." Every day for thirty days, he went into his study and prayed in other tongues and enjoyed it. Finally, his wife said to him, "What's happened to you?"

He said, "What do you mean?"

"Well, *something* has happened," she said.

"Is it good or bad?"

"Oh, it's good!"

So he told her, "When I was up at that Episcopalian meeting, I got baptized in the Holy Ghost and spoke with other tongues."

"I want it too!" she said.

He told me that surprised him. But she saw the results! So he prayed with her and she was filled, or baptized, with the Holy Spirit, and spoke in other tongues. But he didn't tell his church. He waited. And after ninety days, people began to ask him, "What's happened to you?"

"Oh, has something happened to me?" he asked.

"Yes, something's happened to you."

"Is it good or bad?"

"Oh, it's good!"

"What do you mean?" he asked.

They said, "You're preaching is more powerful. You just have more power about you."

So many people asked that this Methodist pastor finally announced he would speak the next Sunday morning on what had happened to him. The day came, and he related his experience.

Now this was quite a large Methodist church. One businessman in that church was the biggest financial contributor. Usually, whichever way he went on an issue, people followed him. The pastor knew if that businessman came up to be baptized in the Holy Spirit, everyone else would be all right with it. So the minister related in detail what had happened to him. Then he asked, "How many of you want this experience? How many would like to be baptized in the Holy Spirit?"

That pastor told me that, without hesitation, the businessman jumped up and said, "I do!" He came forward, and two-thirds of the church followed him down the aisle. They'd seen the results of that experience!

More Power

I remember preaching during the 1950s in the First Assembly of God in West Columbia, Texas, for Brother B. B. Hankins. One night after the service, a visiting Presbyterian pastor was at the parsonage with us having some refreshments. He and Brother Hankins told me that they had gone together to Houston to a Full Gospel Business Men's Fellowship meeting. During that meeting, another Presbyterian minister gave his testimony of being filled with the Holy Spirit. So this Presbyterian fellow went forward and was baptized with the Holy Ghost and spoke with tongues.

The church this Presbyterian fellow pastored had no Sunday night service, but eight or ten members would meet on Sunday nights for coffee and donuts. After this minister was baptized in the Holy Spirit, he started having Sunday night evangelistic services. (The baptism in the Holy Spirit will make you a witness!) This Presbyterian minister started getting people born again, and the church increased. Then he started dealing privately with people whom he saw were hungry for God. People would come and ask him questions, and he'd pray with them in the parsonage. Finally, they had more than thirty people baptized with the Holy Ghost.

But you can't keep that kind of thing a secret for long. During a board meeting at this pastor's church, one of the board members brought the issue up and wanted the pastor dismissed because he was talking in tongues and getting some members of the congregation filled with the Holy Ghost too.

But one of the most influential board members spoke up. He was one of the leading businessmen of that city and the main contributor to that church. He said, "I don't have this experience, but, men, wait just a minute. This fellow has been here for five years. We've listened to him preach for five years *without* this experience, and we've heard him preach *with* this experience. He's got more power now. He's more dynamic. In fact, I'm reluctant to say this in front of his face, but it used to be a bore for me to come and hear him. But now I enjoy every service!"

This board member continued, "Our pastor is getting people saved, the church is growing, and our finances are up. Instead of talking about dismissing him, we ought to talk about keeping him and increasing his salary." So they voted to increase his salary substantially!

This Presbyterian pastor told me, "Boy, being baptized with the Holy Ghost not only enhanced me spiritually, it paid off for me financially. They raised my pay!"

The people in that Methodist church and that Presbyterian church were wise. They saw the difference in their pastors *before* they were baptized in the Holy Spirit, and *after*.

Led the Same Way

Well, when I was baptized in the Holy Ghost, I was led the same way those two pastors were led. I didn't tell my congregation, "I'm filled with the Holy Ghost. I speak with other tongues now." I just kept on preaching. And after about thirty days, people began to ask me, "What's happened to you?"

"Has something happened to me?" I'd respond.

"Oh, yes!"

"Well, is it good or bad?"

"Oh, it's good!"

"What do you mean?"

"Well, you're a better preacher than you used to be."

Now I couldn't tell that I was preaching any better. But I'd say, "What do you mean, I'm a better preacher?"

"You have more power. When you preach now, it's solid. It's got a punch to it. Sometimes it almost knocks us off the pew!"

That didn't mean I preached hard. But there was *power* in those words, praise God! And when I told the congregation what had happened to me, ninety-three percent of them followed me in and were baptized in the Holy Ghost. We didn't lose anyone. The other seven percent wanted that experience, but they wouldn't pay the price. There is a little price to pay. You have to humble yourself. The ones who didn't receive that experience wouldn't come forward to seek or ask for prayer.

'Something Happened'

I particularly remember Mr. R. O. Cox, a fine Methodist gentleman and a leader in the community. At that time he was eighty-nine years of age and a large landowner. In fact, he, his brother, and another fellow were the wealthiest people in the community.

I was just a teenager when I started preaching, and Mr. R. O. called me "Brother Kenneth." Once as we spoke, he mentioned the name of another large land-owner, Mr. Curry, who had just returned from a tour of Europe with his wife. They were Presbyterians. With their grown children, they made up about five families altogether.

Before I received this experience of the baptism in the Holy Spirit, a Pentecostal family moved into the community. News spread that they talked in tongues, and this Mr. Curry said, "I'll tell you, if that tongue-talking ever gets into this church, I'm pulling my family out." He really meant he'd pull *five* families out.

Now I was baptized in the Holy Ghost while Mr. Curry was gone, and when he returned, I still hadn't announced it publicly. I'd only talked to Mr. Cox. He'd asked me what had happened to me, and I told him. He said, "I thought so. My daughter received that experience several years ago, and I could see a difference in her. When I heard you preach, I thought, *That's it. Our little preacher's been baptized in the Holy Ghost and speaks with tongues.*"

Now our church was out in the country, at a bend in the road. At that spot there was just one general store and the building where we had services. Mr. Cox said he saw Mr. Curry at the store and Mr. Curry asked him, "What's happened to our little preacher while I was gone?"

"Oh, did something happen to him?" Mr. Cox asked.

"Yes, something happened to him," said Mr. Curry.

"Well, is it good or bad?"

"Oh," said Mr. Curry, "it's good!"

"What do you mean, 'What's happened to him?'" asked Mr. Cox.

"He preaches better than he used to," said Mr. Curry.

"Oh, does he?" asked Mr. Cox.

"Oh, yes!" replied Mr. Curry.

Mr. Cox said he just played along with Mr. Curry and told him that he didn't notice much change. Mr. Curry said, "Yes, he's much more powerful in every way than he used to be."

Mr. Cox told me that he thought he'd better tell Mr. Curry about my being baptized with the Holy Ghost before I announced it publicly, because of what Mr. Curry had said in the past about speaking with tongues. So Mr. Cox said to Mr. Curry, "Do you know what happened to our little preacher while you were gone?"

"No, but I know something did."

Mr. Cox continued, "He received the baptism in the Holy Ghost with the evidence of speaking in other tongues!"

Mr. Curry dropped his head. Mr. Cox thought Mr. Curry might be getting ready to say he was pulling his family out of church. Mr. Curry didn't say anything for about ten seconds, but Mr. Cox said it seemed like ten minutes.

When Mr. Curry looked up, he had tears in his eyes. He said to Mr. Cox, "I'll tell you one thing. It makes a believer out of me. I'm a candidate for that experience!"

Glory to God! I believe the baptism in the Holy Ghost *ought* to make a difference! That should be true in the same way that the Holy Ghost coming into a person's heart at the New Birth should make a difference in his or her life. The prophet Ezekiel said, *"A new heart also will I give you, and a new spirit will I put within you . . ."* (Ezek. 36:26). One's spiritual nature is changed when he or she is born again, and the change ought to be obvious to all. But the baptism of the Holy Ghost ought also to be an experience that changes one in such a way that people can see the difference!

Jesus said, *"But ye shall receive power, after that the Holy Ghost is come upon you: and ye shall be witnesses unto me . . ."* (Acts 1:8). We witness vocally, but I'm of the opinion that the greatest way to witness is just to produce the fruits! Let people see something!

CHAPTER TEN

WITNESSING TO YOUR IMMEDIATE FAMILY ABOUT THE BAPTISM IN THE HOLY SPIRIT |

In witnessing to your immediate family, the Lord may lead you differently from the way He has led me, and that's all right. But I know in dealing with my mother, my sister and brothers, my grandmother and grandfather on my mother's side, and my mother's sister and brother, I never said one word to them about God or Jesus. I never tried to get them saved. I didn't even invite them to come hear me preach. I seemed to be led *not* to. Something just held me from it.

I told myself, *I just believe that when they see the reality of being born again, they'll all want it.* And every single one of them followed me in. Every single one of them was born again. They saw the reality of it!

The same thing should be true of the baptism in the Holy Ghost. It's not just an experience for me to receive something to have a big time and enjoy. It is an enduement of power for service! And people should see the difference in my service after I'm baptized with the Holy Spirit.

Let's examine some scriptures on the baptism with the Holy Ghost—the enduement of power from on high.

Let's see what transpired on the Day of Pentecost.

ACTS 2:1–4
1   And when the day of Pentecost was fully come, they were all with one accord in one place.
2   And suddenly there came a sound from heaven as of a rushing mighty wind, and it filled all the house where they were sitting.
3   And there appeared unto them cloven tongues like as of fire, and it sat upon each of them.
4   And they were all filled with the Holy Ghost, and began to speak with other tongues, as the Spirit gave them utterance.

Notice that this experience is called here "filled with the Holy Ghost." John prophesied, *"I indeed baptize you with water unto repentance: but he that cometh after me is mightier than I, whose shoes I am not worthy to bear: he shall baptize you with the Holy Ghost, and with fire"* (Matt. 3:11; see also Luke 3:16).

Looking at this experience from the standpoint of what *Jesus* does, one is *baptized* with the Holy Ghost. Looking from the standpoint of the believer, one *receives* the Holy Ghost, or *is filled with* the Holy Ghost.

As I said earlier, discussing Bible subjects is like climbing a mountain. When you climb up the north side of that mountain, you have one view. When you climb up the south side, you get an entirely different view. Yet it's still the same mountain. In discussing

Bible doctrines and Bible subjects, the same thing is true. The view you have depends on which side of the mountain you climb.

"Which view is right—the north side or the south side?" you may ask. Both of them are correct. Your view changes according to which side you're on. But when you get up on *top* of the mountain, you can see in *all* directions!

Different Manifestations

Now I want to call your attention to something. As we read through The Acts of the Apostles, whenever anyone received this Pentecostal experience after the Day of Pentecost, no further reference is made to a rushing mighty wind, though that could and might happen. Nothing more is said about cloven tongues like as of fire appearing and sitting upon believers. But the Scriptures do refer to believers speaking with tongues.

These other spectacular manifestations might accompany the baptism in the Holy Ghost, or they might not. *But one would expect speaking with tongues to accompany this experience because it repeatedly did in the Book of Acts.*

Now, that doesn't preclude the appearance of the other manifestations or signs. It simply means that tongues always accompanied the experience of the baptism in the Holy Ghost. Cloven tongues of fire and other signs didn't always follow this experience.

However, the following experience happened to me several times.

While pastoring my last church, I was invited to preach at a fellowship meeting in an Assemblies of God church in east Texas. I preached at the eleven o'clock service. God had given me a special message, and I finished up around noon. The pastor and the presbyter of the region were sitting on the platform.

As I closed my message, the Spirit of God inspired me to speak with tongues. I gave what we call a message in tongues or, more scripturally, an utterance in tongues, and the pastor stood up and interpreted it. Then I spoke with tongues again under the inspiration of the Spirit, and the pastor again stood up and interpreted it.

The Wind of the Spirit

Now the building was full—just jam-packed. There may have been a few people standing in the back. And when that pastor interpreted the second message, there was a sound just like a wind blowing. Whoosh! Everyone heard it. You could feel it blow right through that building.

We never prayed for anyone or laid hands on anyone, but every sick person in that building was instantly healed! One woman had been brought by ambulance to the meeting and rolled in on a stretcher, and the stretcher with her still lying on it had been placed against the wall. I learned later that she'd been operated on six times. She looked like a corpse—the very picture of death. Doctors had said they wouldn't operate on her again. They said, "There's nothing else we can do. She should already be dead."

I never will forget what happened next, because I saw it. When that wind swept through the building, no one touched her. She leaped off that stretcher, ran down the aisle, and was instantly healed!

Now this was an Assemblies of God fellowship meeting, held mainly for pastors and others of that denomination. I learned later, though, that some people who hadn't been baptized in the Holy Ghost were there. And when that wind blew, every person in the building who didn't have the baptism of the Holy Ghost received that experience!

Some sinners were there too. One woman had invited her unsaved neighbor to come. I held a revival in that church the following month, and that neighbor testified: "I thought I was saved because I belonged to a certain church. I joined it when I was a little girl. But if I'd ever been born again, I didn't know it. Whenever the woman who brought me to that meeting last month would talk to me about being born again, I'd say, 'I belong to the church. I'm all right.' But I had no idea what she was talking about.

"During the service, I was sitting next to the aisle with my neighbor. And when that wind blew through, I was born again, baptized with the Holy Ghost, started talking in tongues, and was instantly delivered from smoking cigarettes!"

More than once I have both heard and felt that wind blowing. At other times, I didn't hear anything, but I felt it, and so did others. In this case, it came as a mighty wind. At other times, it just seemed like a gentle wind blowing. When believers are baptized in the Holy Ghost, they may or may not have that experience, but they should *always* expect the manifestation of speaking with tongues.

More Evidence

Now let's look at several other passages of Scripture that refer to receiving the baptism in Holy Spirit. In Acts chapter 8, we read of the Samaritans having that experience.

ACTS 8:5–8,12,14–15
5   Then Philip went down to the city of Samaria, and preached Christ unto them.
6   And the people with one accord gave heed unto those things which Philip spake, hearing and seeing the miracles which he did.
7   For unclean spirits, crying with loud voice, came out of many that were possessed with them: and many taken with palsies, and that were lame, were healed.
8   And there was great joy in that city. . . .
12 But when they believed Philip preaching the things concerning the kingdom of God, and the name of Jesus Christ, they were baptized, both men and women. . . .

14 Now when the apostles which were at Jerusalem heard that Samaria had received the word of God, they sent unto them Peter and John:

15 Who, when they were come down, PRAYED FOR THEM, THAT THEY MIGHT RECEIVE THE HOLY GHOST.

Now, even though the Holy Spirit is at work in the New Birth and comes into believers at that time, we don't call the New Birth "receiving the Holy Spirit." The New Birth is called "receiving Christ." According to Acts 8:5, Philip preached *Christ* to the Samaritans. He didn't preach the Holy Spirit to them. The Holy Spirit is not mentioned until verse 15. (Yet you still can see Him at work before then. Look at the miracles Philip wrought, and the unclean spirits being cast out.)

Verse 14 says, *"Now when the apostles which were at Jerusalem heard that Samaria had received THE WORD OF GOD . . . ."* And we looked in an earlier chapter at First Peter 1:23: *"Being born again, not of corruptible seed, but of incorruptible, BY THE WORD OF GOD, which liveth and abideth for ever."* Acts 8:14 says the Samaritans had received the Word of God. So, according to First Peter 1:23, they were born again by that Word, weren't they? And Jesus said, *". . . that which is born of the Spirit is spirit"* (John 3:6). So these Samaritans were born of the Spirit, though the Spirit isn't mentioned until later.

We don't pray for sinners to receive the Holy Ghost. We pray with them to receive Christ. And when they receive Christ, the Spirit of Christ—which is the Holy Spirit, of course—comes into their hearts. That has to be so, because Paul said, "*. . . if any man have not the Spirit of Christ, he is none of his*" (Rom. 8:9).

A Dual Working

I want you to see the *dual working* of the Holy Spirit here. The apostles and the other members of the early Church believed that being baptized with the Holy Ghost—or, as it's recorded in Acts 8:15, receiving the Holy Ghost—was an experience *subsequent* to salvation.

Were these Samaritans saved? Well, didn't Jesus tell His disciples, "*. . . Go ye into all the world, and preach the gospel to every creature. He that believeth and is baptized shall be saved . . .*" (Mark 16:15–16)? And we just read that these Samaritans believed and were baptized. So according to what Jesus said, they were saved.

And we have another witness. According to Peter, these Samaritans were saved. Acts 8:14 says, "*Now when the apostles which were at Jerusalem heard that Samaria HAD RECEIVED THE WORD OF GOD, they sent unto them Peter and John.*" Who is the Word of God? Jesus is the Word of God (John 1:1,14). Jesus is the Living Word (1 Peter 1:23). These Samaritans had received Jesus then, hadn't they? They had received Christ.

Now Acts 8:15 says that when Peter and John came down, they prayed for the Samaritans. For what purpose?

Did they pray that these Samaritans might be born again—that they might be converted and become Christians? No. They prayed for them, *". . . that they might receive the Holy Ghost."*

Luke, the writer of the Books of Acts, didn't say the Holy Ghost wasn't present already in Samaria, because He *was* present. He must have been there, because Philip was full of the Holy Ghost. We know that, because Philip was one of the men chosen to wait on tables for the disciples in Jerusalem. The Apostles told the other disciples, *"Wherefore, brethren, look ye out among you seven men of honest report, FULL OF THE HOLY GHOST . . ."* (Acts 6:3). So the Holy Spirit was at work in Samaria before Peter and John came down from Jerusalem.

Jesus told His disciples, *". . . I am with you alway . . ."* (Matt. 28:20), and, *". . . I will never leave thee, nor forsake thee"* (Heb. 13:5). So when Philip arrived in Samaria, Jesus was there too. He was not there in His flesh and bone body, but in the Person of the Holy Spirit.

So we know that before Peter and John arrived in Samaria, the Holy Spirit was already there and at work. He's the One Who recreated the spirits of the Samaritans when they received the Word of God. He caused them to become new creatures in Christ.

Now look at verse 16: *"For as yet he* [the Holy Ghost] *was fallen UPON none of them . . . ."* Remember that Jesus said, *". . . ye shall receive power, after that the Holy Ghost is come UPON you . . ."* (Acts 1:8). But according to Acts 8:16, *". . . as yet he was fallen upon none of them: only they were* [water] *baptized in the name of the Lord Jesus."*

In verse 17 we read, *"Then laid they their hands on them, and they RECEIVED the Holy Ghost."* They received this experience of the baptism in the Holy Ghost, subsequent to salvation.

Dear friend, let's examine Bible evidence, not church doctrine, to determine whether the New Birth and the baptism in the Holy Spirit are two different experiences. We have clearly seen from the Scriptures that they are.

Getting Acquainted With Jesus

Here is another verse along this line.

ACTS 9:17
17 And Ananias went his way, and entered into the house; and putting his hands on him said, Brother Saul, the Lord, even Jesus, that appeared unto thee in the way as thou camest, hath sent me, that thou mightest receive thy sight, and be filled with the Holy Ghost.

Notice that Ananias called him "Brother Saul." Now before Saul met Christ on the road to Damascus, Saul was in a pretty bad light. He consented to the death of Stephen, the first martyr of the Church (Acts 8:1). He was breathing out threatenings and slaughter against the disciples of the Lord (Acts 9:1). He had in his possession letters from Jewish leaders giving him the authority to put in jail, in bonds and in chains, those who were in that Way (Acts 9:2). You probably wouldn't walk up to a fellow like that and call him "Brother."

But here's another little truth. Ananias said, *". . . Brother Saul, the Lord, even Jesus, that appeared unto thee in the way as thou camest, hath sent me . . ."* (Acts 9:17). In other words, Ananias said, "The One Who sent me is the same Jesus with Whom you became acquainted out there on the road to Damascus." The New Birth is getting acquainted with Jesus. Ananias said Jesus had sent him that Saul might receive his sight. Saul had been blinded by the glory of that light from Heaven mentioned in Acts 9:3. He was not blinded with disease or sickness.

Now notice the rest of Acts 9:17: *". . . Brother Saul, the Lord, even Jesus . . . hath sent me, that thou mightest receive thy sight, AND BE FILLED WITH THE HOLY GHOST."* That's the same experience the Samaritans had when Peter and John laid hands on them.

So through these scriptural examples, Jesus Himself, the Head of the Church, tells us that receiving or being baptized with the Holy Ghost is an experience subsequent to becoming acquainted with Him, or being born again.

Now Acts chapter 9 doesn't say that Paul talked with tongues, but we know he did. He told us he did. He said, *"I thank my God, I speak with tongues more than ye all"* (1 Cor. 14:18). When did Paul start talking with tongues? Like the rest of the disciples, he must have spoken in tongues when he was filled with the Holy Ghost.

Using solid biblical evidence, we can see that the baptism in the Holy Spirit with the evidence of speaking in other tongues is a separate and distinct experience from receiving Christ in the New Birth. And while this experience of receiving Christ is essential to our relationship and walk with God, and to our making Heaven our eternal home, we need to add this deeper dimension to our walk and receive this power that God has provided us for service.

CHAPTER ELEVEN

THE DWELLING PLACES OF THE SPIRIT |

I want us to look at some further Scripture concerning the Holy Spirit. Paul says, *"Know ye not that ye are the temple of God, and that the Spirit of God dwelleth in you?"* (1 Cor. 3:16). That's the *King James* translation. Now notice how much more explicitly this verse reads in *The Amplified Bible.*

1 CORINTHIANS 3:16 (*Amplified*)
16 Do you not discern and understand that you [the whole church at Corinth] are God's temple (His sanctuary), and that God's Spirit has His permanent dwelling in you [to be at home in you, collectively as a church and also individually]?

Now look at First Corinthians 6:19. Here Paul is writing to individuals: *"What? know ye not that your body is the temple of the Holy Ghost which is in you, which ye have of God, and ye are not your own?"*

In this chapter, I want to talk about your body and the church, both the local church and the Church as a whole, as temples of the Holy Ghost.

Dwelling in Us Individually

In his letters to the Corinthians, Paul had more to say along this line.

2 CORINTHIANS 6:14–16

14 Be ye not unequally yoked together with unbelievers: for what fellowship hath righteousness with unrighteousness? and what communion hath light with darkness?
15 And what concord hath Christ with Belial? or what part hath he that believeth with an infidel?
16 And what agreement hath the temple of God with idols? for ye are the temple of the living God; as God hath said, I will dwell in them, and walk in them; and I will be their God, and they shall be my people.

Let's go over that very carefully. Paul wrote this to the Church at Corinth, and it has both an individual application and a corporate application, an application to the whole body or the whole group.

Paul starts out by telling the Corinthians, *"Be ye not unequally yoked together with unbelievers . . ."* (v. 14). The believer is called a believer; unbelievers are called unbelievers. That's simple enough, isn't it?

". . . What fellowship hath righteousness with unrighteousness? . ." (v. 14). Here the believer is called righteousness. That's who he is, according to Second Corinthians 5:21:

*". . . he hath made him to be sin for us, who knew
no sin; THAT WE MIGHT BE MADE THE RIGH-
TEOUSNESS OF GOD IN HIM."* So in light of that,
Paul asked, *". . . what fellowship hath righteousness
with unrighteousness? . . ."* The believer is called
righteousness; the unbeliever is called unrighteousness.

Paul continues, *". . . and what communion hath
light with darkness?"* (v. 14). The believer is called
light; the unbeliever is called darkness. *"And what
concord hath Christ with Belial? . ."* (v. 15). Notice
that the believer is identified with or referred to as
Christ, and the unbeliever is called Belial.

*". . . Or what part hath he that believeth with an
infidel?"* (v. 15). Again, the believer is called a believer;
the unbeliever is called an infidel. *"And what agreement hath the temple of God with idols? . ."* (v. 16).
The believer is called the temple of God; the unbeliever
is called idols.

Now notice what Paul says next: *". . . for ye are the
temple of the living God; as God hath said, I will dwell*
[that means "live"] *in them, and walk in them; and I
will be their God, and they shall be my people"* (v. 16).
Hallelujah! And it's through the Holy Spirit that God
indwells us and lives in us.

The Amplified Bible renders the last part of Second
Corinthians 6:16 this way: ". . . For we are the temple
of the living God; even as God said, I will dwell in and
with and among them and will walk in and with and
among them, and I will be their God, and they shall be
My people." God indwells each one of us individually,

and the Church collectively. The body of each believer is a temple of God, and the Church—the whole Body of believers—is *the* temple of God.

The same thought is present in that marvelous verse of Scripture in First John chapter four: *"Ye are of God, little children, and have overcome them: because greater is he that is in you, than he that is in the world"* (1 John 4:4).

Your Body Is the House of God

Let's consider first your body as a temple of the Holy Ghost, or your body as the house of God. There are three things I want to touch on here in connection with our New Testament relationship with God. (Remember, according to Hebrews 8:6, we have a better covenant than they had under the Old Testament.)

First, God is for us. Romans 8:31 says, *"If God be for us, who can be against us?"* So just as God protected and blessed His people in the Old Testament, the New Testament affirms that He protects and blesses us too!

God is on my side, and I'm on His side! Friend, if God is for us, and if we'll just learn to let Him have His way with us, then there won't be any failure, because God can't fail! Do you see that?

Of course, we can fail apart from Him. That's the problem. We try, so to speak, to "paddle our own canoe" apart from Him. But to have God for us guarantees success in life. God is not a failure, is He?

Second, the Bible teaches us that God is *with* us. (God was also with Israel in the Old Testament.) And again, if God is *with* us, we're bound to succeed if we cooperate with Him and let Him have His way with us. If we try to walk separate from Him, then we won't have His help. But, thank God, He is our Helper; He is *with* us!

Now God was *with* Israel and God was *for* Israel, just as He is with and for us today. But here's where our covenant is better than theirs: *Third*, God also is *in* us!

In the Old Testament, God's people built Him a house to live in. They started by building a tabernacle, and finally they built God a temple, a house. But in that tabernacle and that temple, the Presence of God only dwelled in the Holy of Holies. The Jews called that Divine Presence "the Shekinah glory." No one, not even the High Priest, dared approach that Presence except under the right circumstances, or he would fall dead instantly.

It was required of every male that he present himself at least once a year before the Presence of God in the temple. But under the *New* Covenant, God no longer dwells in a man-made Holy of Holies! He lives in each believer all the time!

Sometimes we call a church building the house of God. If we mean that the building is God's house because God dwells there, we are wrong. If we mean that we built it for His glory and will use it as a sanctuary in which to worship Him, that's fine.

The building belongs to us. But, you see, God doesn't indwell that building. He indwells the Body of

Christ, His Church, which is now His temple. And He also indwells us individually.

'It Is Finished'

A remarkable thing happened when Jesus died on the Cross. Jesus cried out, "It is finished!" (See John 19:30.) Some people mistakenly say that He meant the plan of redemption was finished. No, the plan of redemption wasn't finished until after Jesus died, rose from the dead, and ascended into the heavenly Holy of Holies, as the Book of Hebrews tells us, to obtain an eternal redemption for us with His own blood. (See Hebrews 9:12.)

What did Jesus mean, then, when He said, "It is finished"? Check the Scriptures very carefully and you'll find out that when Jesus said, "It is finished" and gave up His spirit, the curtain in the temple that had partitioned off the Holy of Holies and kept God's Presence shut up was rent in twain from top to bottom. (See Matthew 27:50,51; Mark 15:37,38; Luke 23:45,46; and John 19:30.)

The scriptural accounts don't say that the temple veil was rent in twain, or torn in two, from *bottom* to *top*. They say it was rent from *top* to *bottom*. Some unseen being—an angel of God twenty feet up in the air—had to have taken hold of that veil with his hands and ripped it apart downward. And God would never again dwell within a man-made Holy of Holies. He would indwell the believers, the Body of Christ!

The Shekinah glory, that Divine Presence, is not only for us and with us as it was for and with Israel, but it is *in* us! Hallelujah! *". . . Greater is he that is in you, than he that is in the world"* (1 John 4:4). That verse sends a thrill through my spirit every time I say it. My! If we ever realized *Who* is in us, and *what* is in us, and the power available to us, we'd take off like a rocket!

I found out that when I hit the hard places in life, if I'll just stand still in the midst of the storm and speak out calmly, "Greater is He that is in me, than he that is in the world," I'll come through in victory.

We all hit hard places in life, dear friend. None of us is immune. The crises of life come to all of us, because Satan is the god of this world (1 Cor. 4:4). We're surrounded by darkness. If nothing else, the devil will put pressure on you. You'll face the crises of life. We all face the same trials and tests.

But remember, dear friend: the Holy Spirit is greater than any test! He's greater than any trial or storm. He's greater than any crisis, any sickness, any disease, any demon, or any evil spirit! The Holy Spirit is the Greater One.

What is the Greater One doing in us? Is He just a spiritual hitchhiker, hitching a ride with us through life? No! Thank God, He's in us to put us over in life. He's in us to help us!

The Role of the Comforter

In John 14:16 Jesus said, *"And I will pray the Father, and he shall give you another Comforter . . . ."* The Greek word "paraclete" in the original text is translated "Comforter" in the *King James Version*. In many other versions, paraclete is translated "Helper." The word literally means *One called alongside to help.* But the Holy Spirit has not only come *alongside* us to help us—He's *in* us.

I like the *Amplified* wording of John 14:16 in which we can see the full meaning of the word translated "Comforter."

> **JOHN 14:16 (*Amplified*)**
> **16 And I will ask the Father, and He will give you another Comforter (Counselor, Helper, Intercessor, Advocate, Strengthener, and Standby), that He may remain with you forever.**

The word translated "Comforter" has all of those meanings. And He's in me! He's in me as a Strengthener. He's in me as a Standby. What does "Standby" mean? Well, you may not need Him so much when everything is going well. But you do need Him "standing by," ready to help when things get tough!

The Standby

I remember a number of years ago, my wife and I were traveling from church to church holding meetings.

We sometimes remained at a church anywhere from three to nine weeks, and we grew tired of staying in motels. So we bought a twenty-six-foot travel trailer to pull along behind our car. We enjoyed that trailer immensely.

Now gasoline didn't cost as much then as it does now. But I was trying to be economical, and so I bought a car with a two-barrel carburetor to tow the travel trailer.

Out on the plains of Kansas, when we were on pretty level ground, we didn't have any problem pulling that trailer. But when we hit the Rockies, it bogged down. The car just had a two-barrel carburetor, and it just didn't have any extra or standby power.

I remember a time when I was pulling the trailer going west before freeways were built. A crew was working on the road, so I had to slow down. When I lost my speed, I had to drive at five miles an hour all the way up that grade. If we started going faster than that, the transmission would jump into a higher gear and the engine would stall. The car just didn't have enough power in the higher gears to pull that trailer. I had to keep the transmission in low, and creep up that mountain at five miles an hour.

So I finally traded that car in and bought one with a four-barrel carburetor. The engine had more horsepower under the hood. Now, when we were pulling that trailer, I couldn't tell any difference out on the plains or on little hills like we have in Oklahoma. But when we hit the Rockies . . . whoooo, boy! I pushed down on that gas pedal, and we went right on up the mountain! We didn't stall out like we did before.

You see, I didn't need that extra power under the hood out on the plains when things were running smooth and there were just a few minor hills. But that power was standing by all the time. It was in there. And when I hit the hard places, when I hit the really big mountains, I just pushed down on the accelerator and went on!

That is what the Scriptures mean when they refer to the Holy Spirit as a Standby. And the Standby is in me! He's standing by in me ready to help me when I hit the "mountains" of life, the tough places and hard spots.

So it doesn't bother me to see the mountains up ahead. When I get there, I know I have the Standby in me. Hallelujah!

As I look back on my life, I remember those times when the Holy Spirit was a Standby to me. There were times when I was hardly conscious that He was in me in the sense that everything was running smooth and lovely. But when I hit the hard spots, He was right there to help me. Thank God for the Standby!

So I'm not afraid when I see storm clouds rising. I know the Standby is on the inside of me, praise God! And "greater is he that is in you, than he that is in the world" (1 John 4:4). When the winds of adversity are blowing, you can look the storm in the face and say, "The Greater One is in me. He'll put me over. He'll see me through. I trust in Him!"

CHAPTER TWELVE

THE CHURCH AS THE TEMPLE OF THE HOLY GHOST |

We've seen that, as individual believers, our bodies are temples of the Holy Ghost. But now I want to look at the local church and the Church at large, the entire Body of Christ, as temples of the Holy Ghost. Here again is First Corinthians 3:16 from *The Amplified Bible.*

1 CORINTHIANS 3:16 (*Amplified*)
16 Do you not discern and understand that you [THE WHOLE CHURCH AT CORINTH] are God's temple (His sanctuary) . . . ?

In connection with that, look at Hebrews chapter 3.

HEBREWS 3:1–6
1   Wherefore, holy brethren, partakers of the heavenly calling, consider the Apostle and High Priest of our profession [the original Greek language says *confession*], Christ Jesus;
2   Who was faithful to him that appointed him, as also Moses was faithful in all his house.

3   For this man was counted worthy of more glory than Moses, inasmuch as he who hath builded the house hath more honour than the house.
4   For every house is builded by some man; but he that built all things is God.
5   And Moses verily was faithful in all his house, as a servant, for a testimony of those things which were to be spoken after;
6   But Christ as a son over his own house; WHOSE HOUSE ARE WE, if we hold fast the confidence and the rejoicing of the hope firm unto the end.

Now look in First Timothy chapter 3.

1 TIMOTHY 3:15
15   But if I tarry long, that thou mayest know how thou oughtest to behave thyself IN THE HOUSE OF GOD, WHICH IS THE CHURCH OF THE LIVING GOD, the pillar and ground of the truth.

We're talking about God's house. Under the New Covenant, it's the Church. (Remember, First Corinthians 12:27 and 28 say, *"Now ye are the body of Christ, and members in particular. And God hath set some IN THE CHURCH . . . ."*)

So then, going back to First Corinthians chapter 3 in *The Amplified Bible*, we see the following.

1 CORINTHIANS 3:16 (*Amplified*)
16   Do you not discern and understand that YOU

[the whole church at Corinth] are God's temple (His sanctuary), and that God's Spirit has His permanent dwelling in you [to be at home in you, collectively as a church and also individually]?

Dwelling in Us Collectively

We've looked a little bit at the Holy Spirit dwelling in us as believers *individually*. Now let's consider His dwelling in us as believers *collectively*. According to *The Amplified Bible*, in First Corinthians 3:16, Paul addressed the whole Church at Corinth. There were other buildings in Corinth, but Paul wasn't talking about a man-made building. *Wherever a body of believers gathers together, they are God's temple.*

Jesus said, *". . . if two of you shall agree on earth as touching any thing that they shall ask, it shall be done for them of my Father which is in heaven. For where two or three are gathered together in my name, THERE AM I IN THE MIDST OF THEM"* (Matt. 18:19–20). Well, we know that He's in us as individual believers because the Scripture says, *". . . Christ in you, the hope of glory"* (Col. 1:27). But on the other hand, He's in the midst of us collectively as a church, a body of believers. That reminds me again of Second Corinthians 6:16 in *The Amplified Bible*.

2 CORINTHIANS 6:16 *(Amplified)*
16 What agreement [can there be between] a temple of God and idols? For we are the temple of the living

God; even as God said, I will dwell in and with AND AMONG THEM and will walk in and with AND AMONG THEM, and I will be their God, and they shall be My people.

For you as an individual believer, your body is a temple of the living God. But we as a church also are a temple of the living God. According to the verse we just read, God said, "I will dwell in them *and among them.*" God is saying, "I will *live* in them and among them."

God wants to manifest Himself in us as individuals, but He also wants to manifest Himself *among* us. There is an anointing in the individual who is born again and filled with the Holy Spirit. And those who are ministry gifts to the Body of Christ have an anointing upon them to stand in a particular office. In the same way, there is, so to speak, a corporate anointing *among* us. When we realize that and cooperate with God and His anointing, great things will happen!

The Corporate Anointing Brings Healing

I remember a time when a particular woman came to our Healing School in Broken Arrow, Oklahoma. She actually stopped in the Tulsa area on her way to the Mayo Clinic in Rochester, Minnesota. Doctors had sent her with all her medical records to the clinic. She had been operated on six months before, and the surgeon accidentally slit her esophagus, so she couldn't swallow. She hadn't swallowed in six months and had lost about ninety pounds.

I saw her sitting in the back of the auditorium in Healing School. She had a tube in her nose and had to be fed liquids through that tube because she couldn't eat.

We later learned that her neck was a solid mass of scars. Doctors had made eleven different incisions, trying to correct her problem. Then the doctors sent her to the Mayo Clinic to see what they could do about it.

In Healing School that day, we moved with the Spirit of God in such a way that His Presence became very real. As I looked across the crowd that day, a manifestation of the glory of God had come into the room, and it looked almost like a fog which hung over the people's heads.

I said to the crowd, "He's here, praise God. Just reach up and take your healing."

I never did lay hands on that woman or pray for her. Later she testified that when I told the people to reach up and take their healing, she said, "Well, I'll just receive healing myself right now. That's it, glory to God, I receive my healing." Then she just reached up and pulled the tube out of her nose.

This woman hadn't had a solid bite of food in six months. After the meeting ended, she went across the street to what was then a Mexican restaurant and ate two Mexican dinners! She was healed! And she testified to that a couple of days later.

Well, she must have been healed. She hadn't had a bite of solid food in her stomach for six months, and she ate two Mexican dinners!

What activated the healing power in that woman to heal her body? The corporate anointing did. That corporate anointing is much greater than the individual anointing. It is much more powerful and strong.

You see, the Holy Spirit is among us. We're often conscious of Him *in* us, and of His manifestation and reality. But we should also be conscious of Him *among* us.

A Physical Manifestation

On that particular day in Healing School, the Presence of God was so thick it seemed as though you could cut it with a knife. It was like a cloud. In the Old Testament, when the glory of God moved into the house of God, that glory looked like a cloud. It filled all the house, and the ministers, or priests, could not stand up to minister. That happened when Solomon's temple was dedicated. That temple was the house of God then, and we're the house of God now.

But notice the secret ingredient, so to speak. Notice what must be done for that glory to fill the house, whether it was that house then or God's house now. You can see it very clearly in Second Chronicles chapter 5.

2 CHRONICLES 5:11–14
11 And it came to pass, when the priests were come out of the holy place: (for all the priests that were present were sanctified, and did not then wait by course:
12 Also the Levites which were the singers, all of them of Asaph, of Heman, of Jeduthun, with their

sons and their brethren, being arrayed in white linen, having cymbals and psalteries and harps, stood at the east end of the altar, and with them an hundred and twenty priests sounding with trumpets:)
13 It came even to pass, AS THE TRUMPETERS AND SINGERS WERE AS ONE, TO MAKE ONE SOUND TO BE HEARD IN PRAISING AND THANKING THE LORD; and when they lifted up their voice with the trumpets and cymbals and instruments of musick, and praised the Lord, saying, For he is good; for his mercy endureth for ever: that then the house was filled with a cloud, even the house of the Lord; 14 So that the priests could not stand to minister by reason of the cloud: for the glory of the Lord had filled the house of God.

Notice in verse 13 that the glory of the Lord filled the house of God "*. . . as the trumpeters and singers were as one, to make one sound . . .*" in praising and thanking the Lord. When the congregation moved together in unity to praise and thank the Lord, the glory of the Lord filled the temple.

Hallelujah! And just as the glory of the Lord filled the house of God at that time, God wants His glory to fill His house now. And sometimes that glory is visible!

Believers' Meetings

During the first twelve years of my ministry, I pastored several churches. It was a custom in the Full Gospel denominations I was with to change pastors pretty often. But there was one particular church I pastored where we'd have services very similar to those we have in our Healing School. Similar things—some spectacular things—happened in that church. It was the only church I was ever able to get to that place spiritually.

A service like that would often happen on a Sunday morning. In those days (about 1939 or 1940), we usually just had our regular church members there on Sunday mornings. We had Sunday School and 11:00 a.m. worship, and very seldom had any visitors.

On Sunday nights, we had evangelistic services and would fill the building up and have people standing outside. When the weather was good, we'd open all the windows. (We didn't have air-conditioning in those days.) At times, it looked like more people were standing outside than there were inside. The double doors at the back of the sanctuary would be open, and I could see people standing all the way to the street, and people were looking in every window. The building was full.

But on Sunday morning, as we say in Texas, there was "nobody there but us chickens"—just our regular members.

I was just twenty-one years old and hadn't had the baptism of the Holy Ghost very long. I realized afterward that the Holy Spirit didn't manifest His Presence because of anything I did. But I was unconsciously yielding to the Holy Ghost.

In those days, Pentecostal people thought you were supposed to give testimonies every time you went to church, and if you didn't, you were backslidden. And a lot of times, we'd call on someone to lead the testimony portion of the service.

But I'd say to them, "I'm not going to call on anyone to lead the testimony time anymore. I'm just going to sit down and turn this over to the Holy Ghost." I called this a "believers' service." I'm thoroughly convinced that even if I pastored a church of 5,000 people, at least once a week, I'd have a believers' service like that.

Now you have to have other kinds of services too. But I'd say, "I'm going to turn this over to the Holy Ghost. If anyone has a chorus you want to sing, just start it off and sing it. If anyone wants to testify, just go ahead and testify. If anyone feels the Spirit of God move on you to give a message, or utterance, in tongues, then give it. And if anyone has the interpretation, or a prophecy, then give that too. If the Spirit of God moves on you to dance, then get up and start dancing. Whatever He prompts you to do, do it. I'm turning this meeting over to the Holy Ghost." And then I'd sit down.

It was my responsibility to keep everything flowing right, because God put me there as the pastor. And if things got out of line, I would get up and take over and straighten it out. But that rarely happened. Usually I would just sit there.

We had some of the most phenomenal services. We had messages in tongues, and interpretations. We sang and worshipped God, praised God, clapped our hands, and praised the Lord. And sometimes half the congregation would dance before the Lord. But those are not the times I remember best. Those are not the times that still stand out in my mind. The times that stand out are the times when the Holy Spirit would manifest His Presence so strongly that no one moved. There was a holy "quiet."

Ordinarily, if the Spirit of God was not moving in some clear way, I'd dismiss the service at twelve o'clock. There was no use in hanging around all day. But sometimes we stayed until 1:30 in the afternoon, and even longer. At times the Presence of God moved into that building until the atmosphere looked foggy. The glory came in, and there was a holy quietness.

We didn't have any children's classes or nurseries in those days; we were all just in one room—the babies and children and everyone else. But sometimes there was such a holy quiet. We'd just sit there for forty-five minutes—sometimes an hour or more. No one said a word. Not a child or a baby cried. They sensed that holy Presence. It seemed as though we were basking in the sunlight of God's love, just soaking it up. No one moved.

We didn't do that every week, or every month, or even every three months. We'd have a variety of meetings. It seemed like they would be different every time. But then, sometimes six months or more down the road, we'd have another service like that, and we'd just sit there. No one would say anything. Not a word! Just a holy silence.

Once during one of those meetings, the husband of one of our members came to pick up his wife. He was unsaved and he'd been off somewhere else and came back in his car to pick her up after the service.

The man said later that he drove into the church parking lot and sat there for a while, but didn't see anyone come out. He rolled the window down but didn't hear anything. He got out of the car and walked up to the church building. He couldn't see through the window, but he got his ear right up against it, and he couldn't hear me preaching. He couldn't hear anything. Everything was quiet. He said he thought, *Well, I know they're not all gone. All the cars are here.* He was a sinner, and he thought maybe the Rapture had taken place and they'd all left!

So the man opened the door and came in. I was sitting on the platform and I saw him when he came in. Everyone else there was a believer—we were all in the family of God. (Of course, not every member of the church was there, but a good many of them were.)

The building was only about half full. So he slipped in and sat down on the back pew in the center section. I was the only one on the platform, and I had my eyes open. (The Bible says to watch and pray, so I was watching and praying!)

This unsaved man sat there for a little while. I think it must have been ten minutes. No one said anything! No one moved! But that Presence was there—the glory of the Lord!

As I watched that fellow, suddenly, he started shaking all over like he was having a chill. He shook for a little bit—just trembling all over. Then he got up and walked down the aisle, still shaking like something was on him, and fell over the altar.

We all just sat there. We didn't move. No one even went down there to pray with him. *We thought, God started it. Let Him finish it.* (Sometimes we jump in and try to help God. We seem to think He can't get the job done without us.)

So we all just sat there, and this fellow wept his way "through" and came up from that altar shouting and saved!

I saw that happen more than once. Ordinarily, sinners didn't come on Sunday mornings. But when they came in, the Presence of God was so powerful that they couldn't stand it.

You see, we had charged the atmosphere. We had worshipped the Lord and praised Him. Oh yes, you can charge the atmosphere! We could do it because the house of God was there. All of us believers collectively were His house. And God indwelt the house. I'm not talking about the building. I'm talking about the body of believers that was present there.

Charging the Atmosphere With God's Presence

Before that meeting, I had said to the congregation, "Anything goes this morning. We came to worship the Lord, and to praise Him. Now tonight, we are coming for a different purpose. Tonight we'll hold an evangelistic service. We are not coming tonight to *get* a blessing; we'll be coming *to be* a blessing. We're not coming tonight to get blessed and get something from God; we're coming to help others—to get them saved."

Now everything doesn't fit in an evangelistic service. We'd have a lot of good singing, because the world likes good singing. We'd have a number of good singers do special songs. People all over town would say, "You've got the best singing down there at your church. You've got the best singers in town!"

But every Sunday night during those evangelistic services, we had people saved, baptized with the Holy Ghost, and healed. It was just a common occurrence— a normal thing. Well, that wasn't always common in every other church I pastored. But it was common in that church because we had charged the atmosphere that morning with the Presence of God. And when we came in that night, that Presence was still there!

How did God's Presence come to fill God's house in the Old Testament? We saw in Second Chronicles 5:13 and 14 that God's Presence filled the house *when they became as one.* They had *unity.* They made *one sound.* But it wasn't one sound in griping and complaining! They made one sound *in praising and thanking the Lord!* The whole congregation was praising and thanking the Lord out loud. And *then* the house was filled with the cloud. *Then* the manifestation of His glory came! Can you see that?

With One Accord

In the Acts of the Apostles, we see that same thing in the Early Church.

ACTS 2:46–47
46 And they, CONTINUING DAILY WITH ONE ACCORD in the temple, and breaking bread from house to house, did eat their meat with gladness [Not sadness. Gladness!] and singleness of heart,
47 Praising God, and having favour with all the people. And the Lord added to the church daily such as should be saved.

Notice verse 46 says, *"And they, continuing daily WITH ONE ACCORD . . . ."* There's that "one accord" situation again. That's why they had such a mighty manifestation of God's Presence.

The Manifestation of God's Glory

Let's look in Acts chapter 16 at a story you're probably familiar with. Paul and Silas were in jail. They'd been whipped. Their backs were bleeding. Their feet were in stocks. They had been put into the inner prison.

ACTS 16:24–26
24 Who [the jailer], having received such a charge, thrust them into the inner prison, and made their feet fast in the stocks.

25 And at midnight Paul and Silas prayed, and sang praises unto God: and the prisoners heard them.
26 And suddenly there was a great earthquake, so that the foundations of the prison were shaken: and immediately all the doors were opened, and every one's bands were loosed.

Notice in verse 25 that *both* Paul and Silas prayed and sang praises unto God. And notice that *the prisoners heard them.* In other words, they weren't quiet about it. *And it was as they sang praises unto God that the manifestation of His glory came!* That old jail shook! Every door flew open, and the stocks fell off their feet.

The jailer thought everyone had escaped. He knew he'd be killed, so he started to fall on his sword and take his own life. But Paul cried out to him, ". . . Do thyself no harm: for we are all here" (v. 28). And the jailer called for a light, and sprang in, and said, ". . . sirs, what must I do to be saved?" (v. 30). That all happened when Paul and Silas began to sing and to praise God!

$\mathcal{G}$OD INHABITS THE PRAISES OF HIS PEOPLE |

There's so much said in both the New Testament and the Old Testament about praising God. God is the same now as He was then, even though He has a different house! The Bible says that God inhabits the praises of His people (Ps. 22:3) and that's the reason we praise Him: He inhabits our praises. And as we offer praises to Him, an atmosphere is created in which the Holy Spirit can manifest His Presence.

Let's look for a moment in the Book of Psalms. In the Hebrew Bible, the 150 psalms are divided into five books corresponding to the first five books of the Bible. These five books of psalms were Israel's prayer and song book.

Notice how much the psalms talk about thanks and giving praise. We'll look at just a few of them.

PSALM 105:1–2
1   O give thanks unto the Lord; call upon his name: make known his deeds among the people.
2   SING UNTO HIM, SING PSALMS UNTO HIM: talk ye of all his wondrous works.

Notice verse 2 says, *"Sing unto him . . . ."* Remember, we read in Acts chapter 16, *". . . at midnight Paul and Silas prayed, and SANG PRAISES UNTO GOD"* (v. 25). Did Paul and Silas sing praises to each other? No! They sang praises unto God in the New Testament, as well as the Old Testament.

Look at the account in Acts chapter 13 of those five brethren at Antioch who were prophets and teachers. Barnabas and Saul were two of them. The Bible says, *"As they ministered to the Lord, and fasted, the Holy Ghost said, Separate me Barnabas and Saul for the work whereunto I have called them"* (v. 2). Ministering to the Lord, what do you suppose those brethren did? Why, they prayed and praised God! They sang praises unto Him!

And notice that *as* they ministered to the Lord, the Holy Ghost spoke. You see, that's the kind of atmosphere in which God can speak to us. That's the kind of atmosphere that brings the manifestation of the Presence of God among us. And we need the manifestation of His Presence *among* us as much as we need it *in* us.

Now look at the beginning of both Psalms 106 and 107.

PSALM 106:1
1   Praise ye the Lord. O give thanks unto the Lord; for he is good: for his mercy endureth for ever.

PSALM 107:1–2
1   O give thanks unto the Lord, for he is good: for his mercy endureth for ever.
2   Let the redeemed of the Lord say so . . . .

First, notice Psalm 107:2. How do the redeemed of the Lord say so? By giving thanks unto the Lord, and crying out, "He is good, and His mercy endureth for ever!" Now look at Psalm 108.

PSALM 108:1–3
1   O God, my heart is fixed [I wish we had some more hearts that were fixed]; **I will sing and give praise, even with my glory.**
2   Awake, psaltery and harp: I myself will awake early.
3   I will praise thee, O Lord, AMONG THE PEOPLE: and I will sing praises unto thee AMONG THE NATIONS.
4   For thy mercy is great above the heavens: and thy truth reacheth unto the clouds.

Notice the psalmist does *not* say, "I will praise thee, O Lord, in quietness, and not let anyone know about it." He says, *"I will praise thee, O Lord, AMONG THE PEOPLE: and I will sing praises unto thee AMONG THE NATIONS"* (v. 3). Now look at how Psalm 111 begins.

PSALM 111:1
1   Praise ye the Lord. I will praise the Lord with my whole heart, IN THE ASSEMBLY OF THE UPRIGHT, AND IN THE CONGREGATION.

The psalmist is praising the Lord in a gathering of believers, and with his whole heart. The next two psalms also begin with praise.

PSALM 112:1
1   Praise ye the Lord. Blessed is the man that feareth the Lord, that delighteth greatly in his commandments.

PSALM 113:1–5
1   Praise ye the Lord. Praise, O ye servants of the Lord, praise the name of the Lord.
2   Blessed be the name of the Lord from this time forth and for evermore.
3   From the rising of the sun unto the going down of the same the Lord's name is to be praised.
4   The Lord is high above all nations, and his glory above the heavens.
5   Who is like unto the Lord our God, who dwelleth on high . . . .

Here are two more passages from Psalms that express praise and thanksgiving to the Lord.

PSALM 117:1–2
1   O praise the Lord, all ye nations: praise him, all ye people [What for?].
2   For his merciful kindness is great toward us: and the truth of the Lord endureth for ever. Praise ye the Lord.

PSALM 118:1–2
1   O give thanks unto the Lord; for he is good: because his mercy endureth for ever.
2   Let Israel now say, that his mercy endureth for ever.

The psalmist's admonition to Israel to publicly acknowledge that God's mercy endures forever applies to us in the Church today too. We in the Church need to say out loud, "His mercy endureth for ever."

Our Praises Please God

We've looked at a number of psalms. Now let's go over toward the end of the Book of Psalms. Let's learn something further about praising God. Remember, the psalmist said, "He inhabits the praises of His people." That means He lives in our praises.

PSALM 146:1–2
1   Praise ye the Lord. Praise the Lord, O my soul.
2   While I live will I praise the Lord: I will sing praises unto my God while I have any being.

PSALM 147:1
1   Praise ye the Lord: for it is good to sing praises unto our God; for it is pleasant; and praise is comely.

PSALM 148:1–7
1   Praise ye the Lord. Praise ye the Lord from the heavens: praise him in the heights.

2   Praise ye him, all his angels: praise ye him, all his hosts.

3   Praise ye him, sun and moon: praise him, all ye stars of light.

4   Praise him, ye heavens of heavens, and ye waters that be above the heavens.

5   Let them praise the name of the Lord: for he commanded, and they were created.

6   He hath also stablished them for ever and ever: he hath made a decree which shall not pass.

7   Praise the Lord from the earth . . . .

PSALM 149:1

1   Praise ye the Lord. Sing unto the Lord a new song, **AND HIS PRAISE IN THE CONGREGATION OF SAINTS.**

Hallelujah! Now, let's look at Psalm 150—the one that closes out the Book of Psalms.

PSALM 150:1

1 Praise ye the Lord. Praise God in his sanctuary . . . .

In this chapter, we've seen that both individual believers *and the church collectively* are God's sanctuary. Remember, First Corinthians 3:16 in *The Amplified Bible* says, "Do you not discern and understand that you [the whole church at Corinth] are God's temple (His sanctuary) . . . ?"

PSALM 150:1–6

1   Praise ye the Lord. Praise God in his sanctuary:
praise him in the firmament of his power.
2   Praise him for his mighty acts: praise him according-
ing to his excellent greatness.
3   Praise him with the sound of the trumpet: praise
him with the psaltery and harp.
4   Praise him with the timbrel and dance: praise him
with stringed instruments and organs.
5   Praise him upon the loud cymbals: praise him
upon the high sounding cymbals.
6   Let every thing that hath breath praise the Lord.
Praise ye the Lord.

Say it out loud: "For the Lord is good, and His
mercy endureth forever." Thank God for His glory!
Thank God for His goodness! Thank God for His
mercy! We need to do a lot of praising, because we're
behind in our praising; we need to catch up!

Singing and Dancing

Let's take another in-depth look at Psalm 149. It
begins, *"Praise ye the Lord. Sing unto the Lord a new
song, and his praise in the congregation of saints. Let
Israel rejoice in him THAT MADE HIM . . ."* (vv. 1,2).
Paraphrasing that language and applying it, the Lord
made the Church. Man didn't make it. God's the One
who built this spiritual house.

Verse 2 continues, *". . . let the children of Zion be
joyful in their King."* Did you know that we're children

of Zion? (See Hebrews 12:22.) Now verse 3: *"Let them praise his name in the dance: let them sing praises unto him with the timbrel and harp."* Did you know that singing and dancing originally belonged to God and His people? The devil stole them and perverted them. Well, let's just not let the devil have them! When the Holy Spirit comes upon a person who begins singing and dancing in the Spirit, it can bring great blessing to a worship service.

Psalm 149 continues, *"Let them praise his name in the dance: let them sing praises unto him with the timbrel and harp. FOR THE LORD TAKETH PLEASURE IN HIS PEOPLE . . ."* (vv. 3,4). What does that mean? It means that the Lord takes pleasure in His people praising Him in the dance. It pleases Him! Some old mulligrub might say, "I don't like it." Well, the devil and his crowd don't, either. But that's all right. *God* does!

The psalmist is talking here about *rejoicing*—about being *joyful*. He talks about praising God's Name in the dance and singing praises unto Him with the timbrel and harp.

PSALM 149:4–6
4   For the Lord taketh pleasure in his people: he will beautify the meek with salvation.
5   Let the saints be joyful in glory: let them sing aloud upon their beds [That means we need to act this way at home too].
6   Let the high praises of God be in their mouth, and a twoedged sword in their hand . . . .

The Word of God is the sword of the Spirit in our hands, but we need to put the high praises of God in our mouths too! That's when His Word will be effective—believing it in our heart and speaking it with our mouth, wielding that Word as a two-edged sword against the tests and trials of life that beset us.

Now the New Testament says, *"And take . . . the sword of the Spirit, which is the word of God"* (Eph. 6:17). The Word of God is our two-edged sword. A lot of people are running around with a Bible in their hand saying, "I'm a Word person," but they look as though they've been eating sour grapes. They never smile, and they have no joy. But Psalm 149:4 says, *". . . he will BEAUTIFY the meek with salvation."* That doesn't sound like those sour-grapes people, does it?

Yes, we need to take the two-edged sword of the Spirit—the Word of God—and wield it with our mouths! But if we're angry and we cut people with it, we don't do any good. No, we need to let the high praises of God be in our mouths. When we do that, we'll use that sword with praise and thanksgiving, and folks will want it!

Deliverance Brings Rejoicing

Let's look at Psalm 137, referring to the time when Israel was held captive in Babylon.

PSALM 137:1–3
1   By the rivers of Babylon, there we sat down, yea, we wept, when we remembered Zion.

2   We hanged our harps upon the willows in the midst thereof.

3   For there they that carried us away captive required of us a song; and they that wasted us required of us mirth, saying, Sing us one of the songs of Zion.

We just read some of the songs of Zion. They were full of joy and praise. Did you notice that? But in Psalm 137, the psalmist goes on to say, *"How shall we sing the Lord's song in a strange land"* (v. 4)? That's why a lot of folks in the church can't sing. They've been living out on the devil's territory, acting and living like the devil.

But look now in Psalm 126 at what happened when the Lord changed that.

PSALM 126:1–3

1   When the Lord turned again the captivity of Zion, we were like them that dream.

2   THEN WAS OUR MOUTH FILLED WITH LAUGHTER, AND OUR TONGUE WITH SING-ING: then said they among the heathen, The Lord hath done great things for them.

3   The Lord hath done great things for us; whereof we are glad.

In Psalm 137 when Israel's captors said, "Sing one of the songs of Zion," they said, "How can we sing one of those joyful songs when we're in captivity?" But when the Lord turned their captivity and delivered Israel from Babylon, they said, "*. . . we were like them that dream. Then was our mouth filled with laughter, and our tongue with singing . . .*" (Ps. 126:1–2). They were glad!

The Mighty Working
of God's Spirit in Praise

In conclusion, let's look in Psalm 29 and learn some things about the working of the Spirit of God. When the psalmist talks about the voice of the Lord here, he is using a type—a symbol. He is talking about the Spirit of God, the Holy Spirit. And the references to many waters, seas, oceans, and so on are types, or symbols, for multitudes of people.

PSALM 29:1–9
1   Give unto the Lord, O ye mighty, give unto the Lord glory and strength.
2   Give unto the Lord the glory due unto his name; worship the Lord in the beauty of holiness.
3   The voice of the Lord is upon the waters: the God of glory thundereth: the Lord is upon many waters.
4   The voice of the Lord is powerful; the voice of the Lord is full of majesty.
5   The voice of the Lord breaketh the cedars; yea, the Lord breaketh the cedars of Lebanon.
6   He maketh them also to skip like a calf; Lebanon and Sirion like a young unicorn.
7   The voice of the Lord divideth the flames of fire.

8　The voice of the Lord shaketh the wilderness; the
Lord shaketh the wilderness of Kadesh.
9　The voice of the Lord maketh the hinds to calve,
and discovereth the forests: and in his temple doth
every one speak of his glory.

The psalmist starts out by telling us to give unto the
Lord glory and strength, and the glory due His Name.
Now look at verse 7: *"The voice of the Lord divideth
the flames of fire."* This verse reminds us of the tongues
of fire in Acts chapter 2 when the Holy Spirit was
poured out upon the Church. Acts chapter 2 says,
*"And when the day of Pentecost was fully come, they
were all with one accord in one place. And suddenly
there came a sound from heaven as of a rushing mighty
wind, and it filled all the house where they were sitting.
AND THERE APPEARED UNTO THEM CLOVEN
TONGUES LIKE AS OF FIRE, and it sat upon each
of them. And they were all filled with the Holy Ghost,
and began to speak with other tongues, as the Spirit
gave them utterance"* (vv. 1–4).

Now look at verse 9: *"The voice of the Lord
maketh the hinds to calve . . . and in his temple doth
every one speak of his glory."*

Remember First Corinthians 3:16 in *The Amplified
Bible* says, "Do you not discern and understand that
you [the whole church at Corinth] are God's temple
(His sanctuary), and that God's Spirit has His permanent dwelling in you [to be at home in you, collectively
as a church and also individually]?" And Psalm 29:9 in

the *King James Version* says, *". . . and in his temple doth every one speak of his glory."* Well, the literal Hebrew there says, *". . . in his temple doth every one say glory."* Why? Because God's glory is present and evident. You see, the Church is God's temple. And in His temple, the *King James Version* says, *". . . doth every one speak of his glory."*

Experiencing the Glory of God

Now let's look at a passage of Scripture in Romans chapter 6 dealing with the glory of God.

ROMANS 6:4
4   Therefore we are buried with him [that's Jesus] by baptism into death: that like as Christ was raised up from the dead by the glory of the Father . . . .

We read about that glory all through the Old Testament. Jesus was raised up by the glory of the Father. Now notice how Romans 8:11 begins: *"But if the Spirit of him that raised up Jesus from the dead . . . ."* So Paul, the writer of Romans, relates the Spirit of God with "the glory of the Father," or the glory of God!

Sometimes you feel or sense the glory of God and sometimes you see it. As we read earlier, the glory of God was manifested in the Old Testament like a cloud (see 2 Chronicles 5:13,14). And in the New Testament, that glory is manifested among us and in us. Now let's read all of Romans 8:11.

ROMANS 8:11
11 But if the Spirit of him that raised up Jesus from the dead dwell in you, he that raised up Christ from the dead shall also quicken your mortal bodies by his Spirit that dwelleth in you.

This verse isn't referring to the resurrection of your body. Your body is not mortal when it's resurrected. Mortal means doomed to death, and if your body is being resurrected, it has already died. This is talking about *now*! "*. . . he that raised up Christ from the dead shall also quicken your mortal bodies by his Spirit that dwelleth in you.*"

God's glory and Spirit are in you! And if the Spirit of God dwells in you, He will quicken your mortal body. "Quicken" means *make full of life*. It doesn't mean to make full of death, sickness, or disease! The Lord will make your mortal body full of life by His Spirit that dwelleth in you!

Individually and Collectively

Let's remember, then, that God's Spirit—the Holy Spirit, or the Holy Ghost—indwells us *individually* as believers, and *collectively* both as a local church and as the whole Church, the whole Body of Christ. The Spirit of God no longer dwells in a house made by hands; He dwells in us!

When we become believers in Jesus Christ, our bodies become temples of the Holy Ghost. He's living in us. He's in us to help us and He'll put us over in life if we'll just learn to cooperate with Him.

It doesn't matter what trial comes our way, because the Greater One lives in us. And *". . . greater is he that is in you, than he that is in the world"* (1 John 4:4).

The Holy Spirit also dwells in us collectively as a Church, a body of believers. He wants to manifest Himself among us and through us to help others. He wants to see the Church blessed, and see sinners saved, healed, and filled with the Spirit. As we in the Church learn to praise and thank the Lord in unity for who He is and what He's done for us, we'll create an atmosphere in which the Holy Ghost can work.

Allow the Spirit To Work Both Within and Upon

The Holy Spirit desires to work fully in our lives. He comes *within* us the moment we are born again and begins to cultivate in us the characteristics of a Christian, the ninefold fruit of the Spirit. Within us, He becomes, as Jesus said, *". . . a well of water springing up into everlasting life"* (John 4:14).

But the Holy Spirit also desires to come *upon* us through the experience of the baptism in the Holy Spirit. He desires to empower us to serve the purposes of Christ in *God's* strength, not our own. He desires to bring us into a deeper spiritual experience than we have with His indwelling Presence alone. He yearns to flow through us to bless mankind as the "rivers of living water" Jesus spoke of in John 7:38. And the

Holy Spirit desires to manifest Himself through us as He wills in the ninefold gifts of the Spirit.

Let's allow God's Holy Spirit to work in our lives not just to bless us, but to empower us *to be* a blessing. Let's allow Him to be in us both a well of spiritual water to satisfy *our* thirst, and rivers of living water flowing through us to meet the needs of *others*! Let's allow Him to work with us as both the Spirit within *and* the Spirit upon!

Why should you consider attending

RHEMA
Bible Training Center?

Here are a few good reasons:

- Training at one of the top Spirit-filled Bible schools anywhere

- Teaching based on steadfast faith in God's Word

- Growth in your spiritual walk coupled with practical training in effective ministry

- Specialization in the area of your choosing:
  Youth or Children's Ministry, Evangelism, Pastoral Care, Missions, or Supportive Ministry

- Optional intensive third-year programs—School of Worship, School of Pastoral Ministry, School of World Missions, and General Extended Studies

- Worldwide ministry opportunities—while you're in school

- An established network of churches and ministries around the world who depend on RHEMA to supply full-time staff and support ministers

Call today for information or application material.
1-888-28-FAITH (1-888-283-2484)
www.rbtc.org

RHEMA Bible Training Center admits students of any race, color, or ethnic origin.

OFFER CODE—BKORD:PRMDRBTC

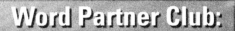

Always on.

For the latest news and information on products, media, podcasts, study resources, and special offers, visit us online 24 hours a day.

www.rhema.org

Free Subscription!

Call now to receive a free subscription to *The Word of Faith* magazine from Kenneth Hagin Ministries. Receive encouragement and spiritual refreshment from . . .

- *Faith-building articles from Kenneth W. Hagin, Lynette Hagin, and others*
- *"Timeless Teaching" from the archives of Kenneth E. Hagin*
- *Feature articles on prayer and healing*
- *Testimonies of salvation, healing, and deliverance*
- *Children's activity page*
- *Updates on RHEMA Bible Training Center, RHEMA Bible Church, and other outreaches of Kenneth Hagin Ministries*

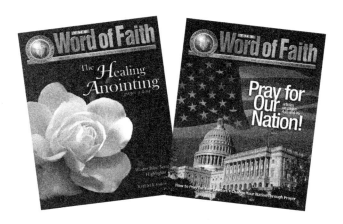

Subscribe today for your free *Word of Faith*!

1-888-28-FAITH (1-888-283-2484)

www.rhema.org/wof

OFFER CODE—BKORD:WF

RHEMA
Correspondence Bible School

The RHEMA Correspondence Bible School is a home Bible study course that can help you in your everyday life!

This course of study has been designed with you in mind, providing practical teaching on prayer, faith, healing, Spirit-led living, and much more to help you live a victorious Christian life!

Flexible
Enroll any time: choose your topic of study;
study at your own pace!

Affordable
Pay as you go—only $25 per lesson!
(Price subject to change without notice.)

Profitable

"The Lord has blessed me through a RHEMA Correspondence Bible School graduate. . . . He witnessed to me 15 years ago, and the Lord delivered me from drugs and alcohol. I was living on the streets and then in somebody's tool shed. Now I lead a victorious and blessed life! I now am a graduate of RHEMA Correspondence Bible School too! I own a beautiful home. I have a beautiful wife and two children who also love the Lord. The Lord allows me to preach whenever my pastor is out of town. I am on the board of directors at my church and at the Christian school. Thank you, and God bless you and your ministry!"

—D.J., Lusby, Maryland

"Thank you for continually offering RHEMA Correspondence Bible School. The eyes of my understanding have been enlightened greatly through the Word of God through having been enrolled in RCBS. My life has forever been changed."

—M.R., Princeton, N.C.

For enrollment information and a course listing, call today!

1-888-28-FAITH (1-888-283-2484)

www.rhema.org/rcbs

OFFER CODE—BKORD:BRCSC